The
Year of *Grace*

A Larger-than-Life Father,
a Pain-in-the-Ass Daughter, and Their
Transformative Journey through Dementia

by

HARRIET BOORHEM, Ed.D.

LESHARKAT
Publishing

DALLAS, TEXAS

Paperback ISBN: 979-8-9881022-0-5
E-book ISBN 979-8-9881022-1-2
Library of Congress Control Number: 2023906138

for my tribe,
Bill, Ann, Beth, Barbra, and Ross,
without whom life would be so dull
and
for my girls,
Kat and Leslie,
without whom I would be lost

with special recognition for
Kevin,
who came to the chaos late and survived

"Life is for the living. Don't waste it!"

WILLIAM BOORHEM

Contents

Family
In Relation to the Author

William Boorhem . . . . . . Daddy / Crusher Bill / Popio / Pops / My Father
Shelby Boorhem, Sr. . . . . Daddy's Father / My Grandfather
Lillian McGillicuddy (Nonna) . . . . . Daddy's Mother / My Grandmother
Frank McGillicuddy . . . . Daddy's Stepfather
Shelby Martin Boorhem . . . . Daddy's Brother / My Uncle
Ross Jesse McCormack . . . . Mother's Father / My Grandfather
Hattye McCormack . . . . Mother's Mother / My Grandmother
Jane McCormack Boorhem . . . . Daddy's First Wife / My Mother
Ann Ross McCormack Rutherford . . . . Mother's Sister / My Aunt
Pat Hamlin Boorhem . . . . Daddy's Second Wife / My Stepmother
Kevin Hamlin . . . . Pat's Son / My Stepbrother
Maria Helena Boorhem . . . . Shelby Martin's Wife / My Aunt
William Martin Boorhem (Bill) . . . . My Older Brother
Ann Ross Boorhem Medlin . . . . My Older Sister
Elizabeth Boorhem Downing (Beth) . . . . . My Older Sister / Barbra's Twin
Barbra Boorhem Heimbach . . . . My Older Sister / Beth's Twin
Harriet Boorhem . . . . Author—Next to Youngest
Shelby Ross Boorhem (Ross) . . . . My Younger Brother

POPIO'S GRANDCHILDREN

Grandchild	*Parent*
Wiley Austin Eli	Bill
Noah William Tyler	Bill
Andrea Beth	Ann
Rebecca Ann	Ann
Sarah Jane	Beth
Orville Ellis III (Bub)	Beth
Katherine Elizabeth	Harriet
Anna Leslie	Harriet
Landry Sue	Kevin

POPIO'S GREAT-GRANDCHILDREN

Great-Grandchild	*Parent*
Beatrice	Wiley
William	Wiley
Alexander	Noah
Emilia Sophia	Noah
Bailey	Andrea
Luke	Andrea
Sebastian	Rebecca
Will	Sarah
Jane	Sarah

Genograms

BOORHEM FAMILY WITH GRANDPARENTS

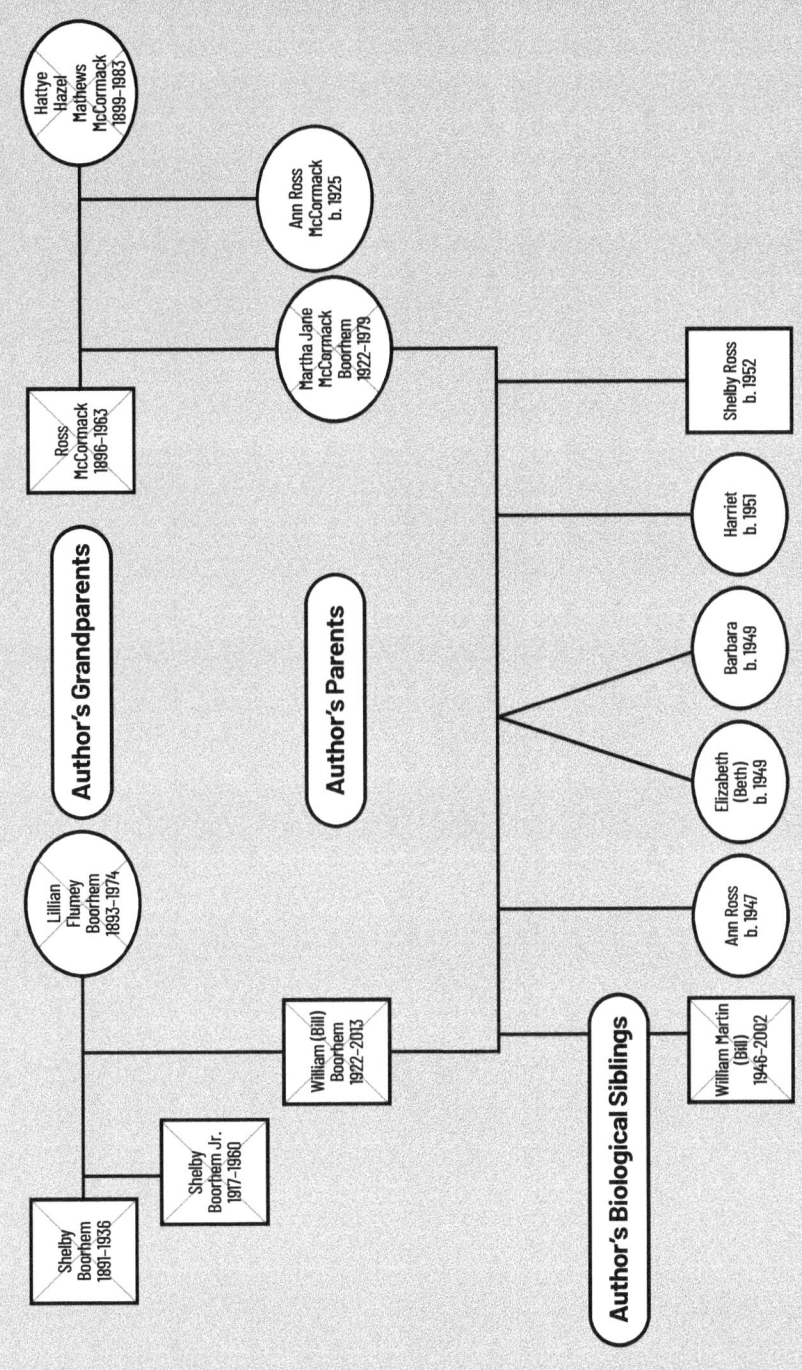

Author's Grandparents

Hattye Hazel Mathews McCormack 1899–1983

Ann Ross McCormack b. 1925

Ross McCormack 1896–1963

Martha Jane McCormack Boorhem 1922–1979

Lillian Flumey Boorhem 1893–1974

Author's Parents

William (Bill) Boorhem 1922–2013

Shelby Boorhem Jr. 1917–1960

Shelby Boorhem 1891–1936

Shelby Ross b. 1952

Harriet b. 1951

Barbara b. 1949

Elizabeth (Beth) b. 1949

Ann Ross b. 1947

Author's Biological Siblings

William Martin (Bill) 1946–2002

BOORHEM—HAMLIN FAMILY POST-1979

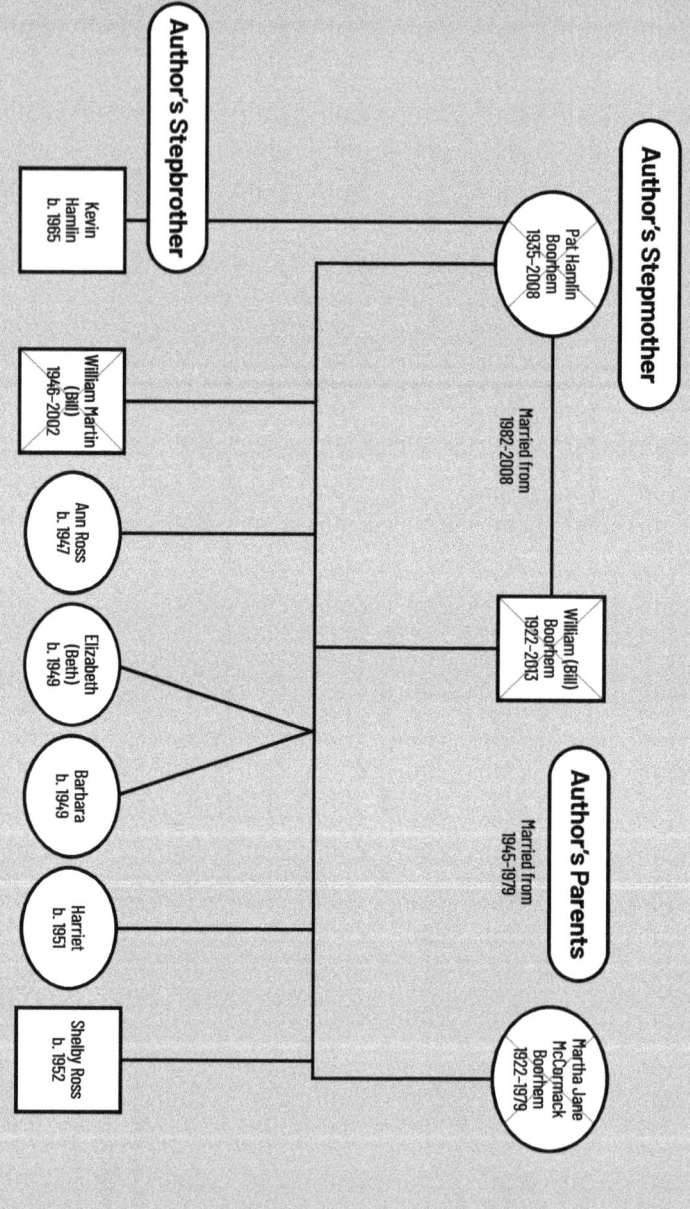

Author's Stepmother

Pat Hamlin
Boorhem
1935-2008

Author's Stepbrother

Kevin
Hamlin
b. 1985

Married from
1982-2008

William (Bill)
Boorhem
1922-2013

William Martin
(Bill)
1946-2002

Ann Ross
b. 1947

Elizabeth
(Beth)
b. 1949

Barbara
b. 1949

Author's Parents

Married from
1945-1979

Harriet
b. 1951

Shelby Ross
b. 1952

Martha Jane
McCormack
Boorhem
1922-1979

BOORHEM — HAMLIN SIBLING FAMILY GROUPS

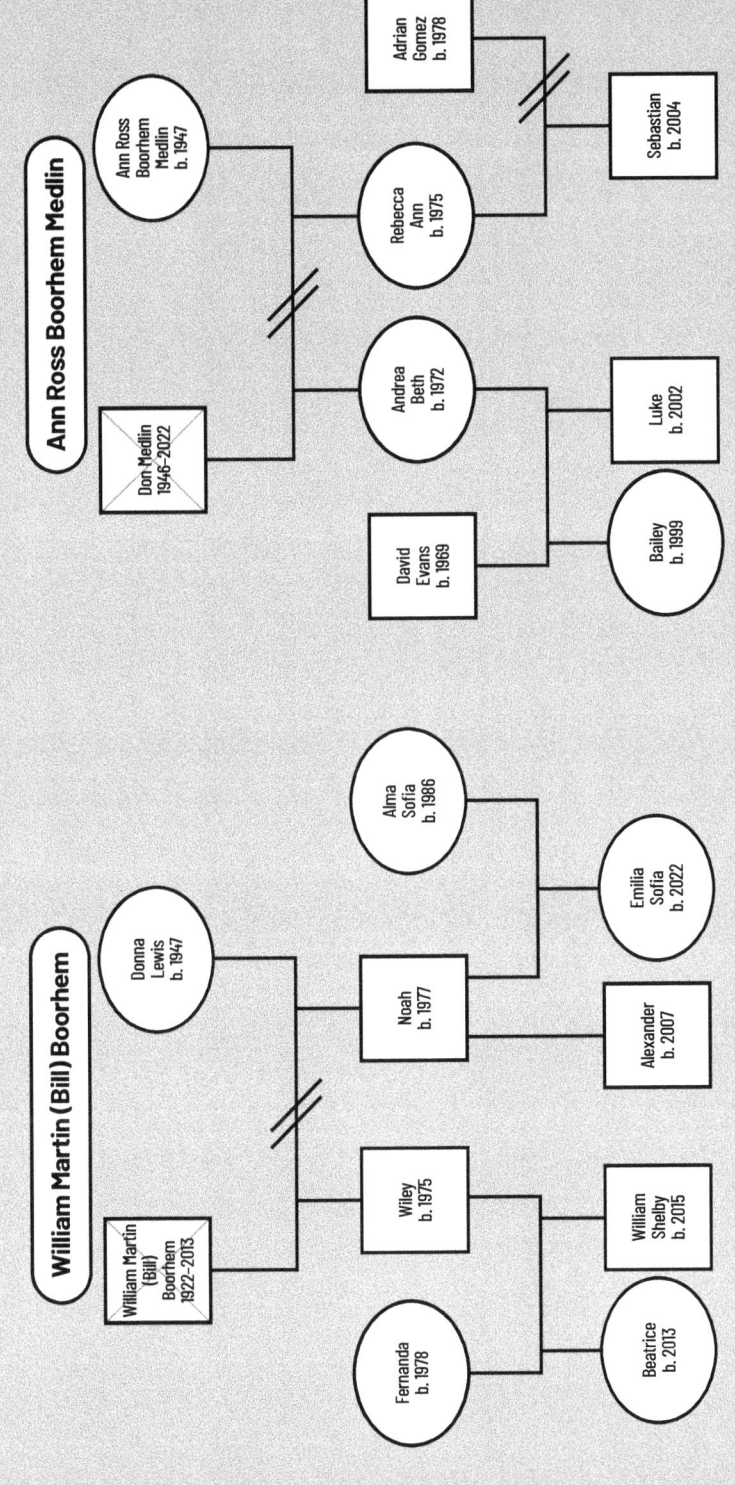

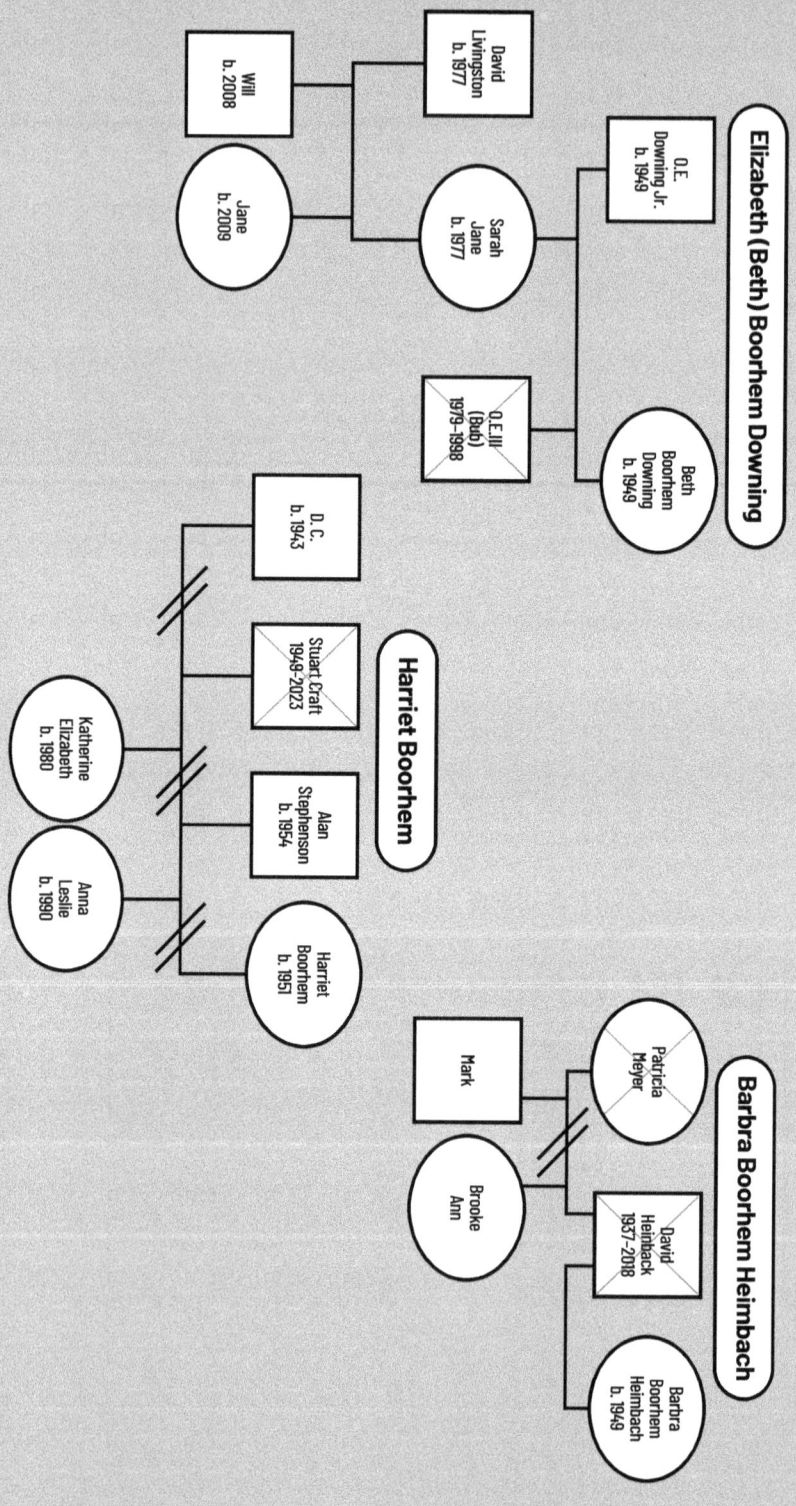

BOORHEM — HAMLIN SIBLING FAMILY GROUPS

Elizabeth (Beth) Boorhem Downing

Will
b. 2008

Jane
b. 2009

David
Livingston
b. 1977

Sarah
Jane
b. 1977

O.E.
Downing Jr.
b. 1949

O.E. III
(Bud)
1979-1998

Beth
Boorhem
Downing
b. 1949

Harriet Boorhem

D.C.
b. 1943

Stuart Craft
1949-2023

Alan
Stephenson
b. 1954

Katherine
Elizabeth
b. 1980

Anna
Leslie
b. 1990

Harriet
Boorhem
b. 1951

Barbra Boorhem Heimbach

Mark

Patricia
Meyer

Brooke
Ann

David
Heimback
1937-2018

Barbra
Boorhem
Heimbach
b. 1949

BOORHEM — HAMLIN SIBLING FAMILY GROUPS

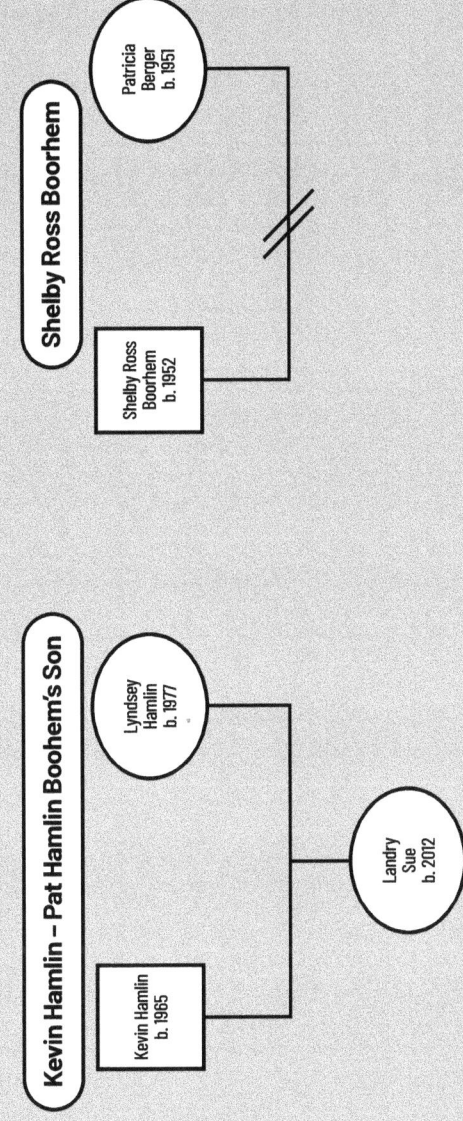

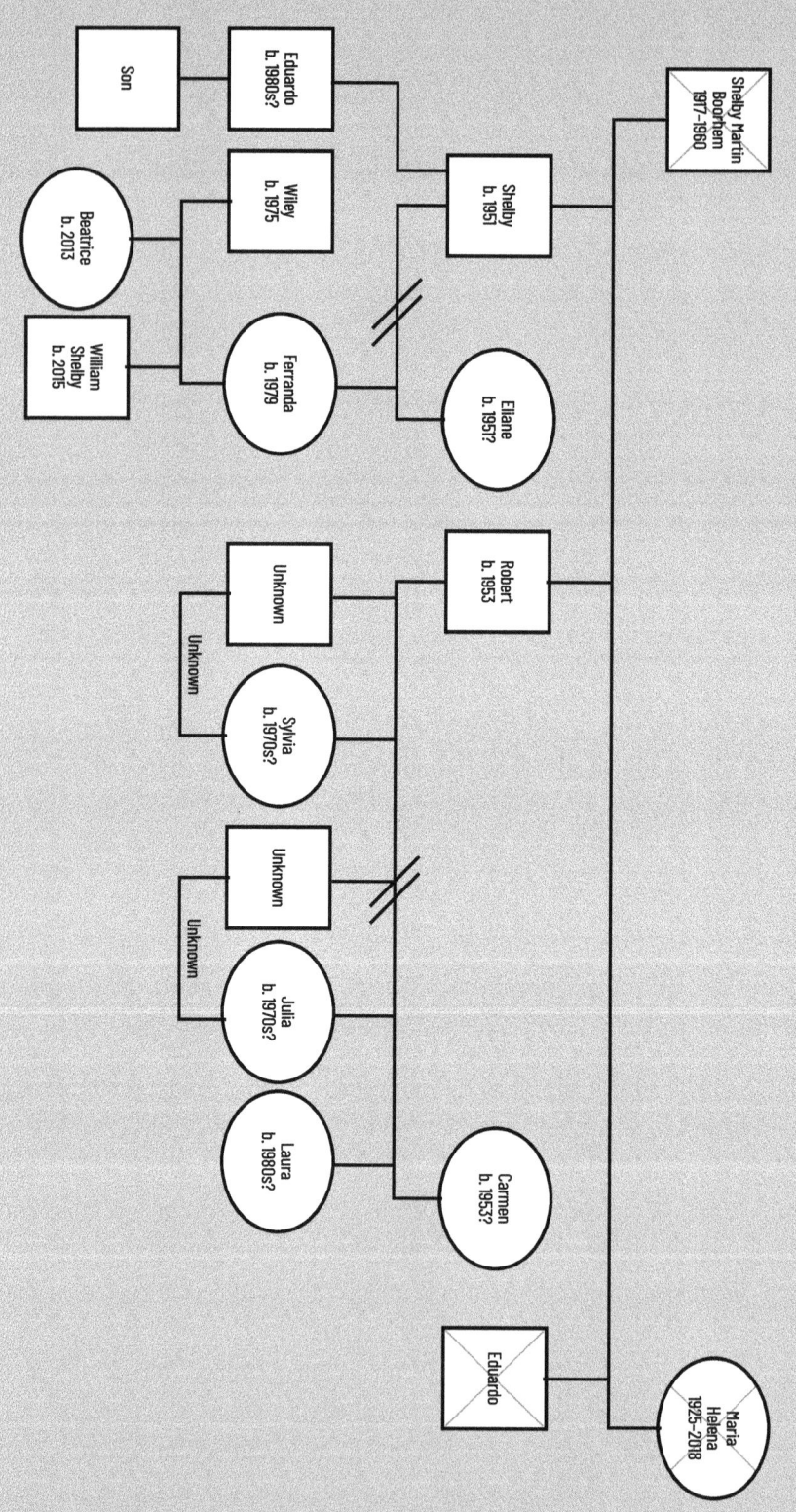

BOORHEM FAMILY IN BRAZIL

Key for Genograms

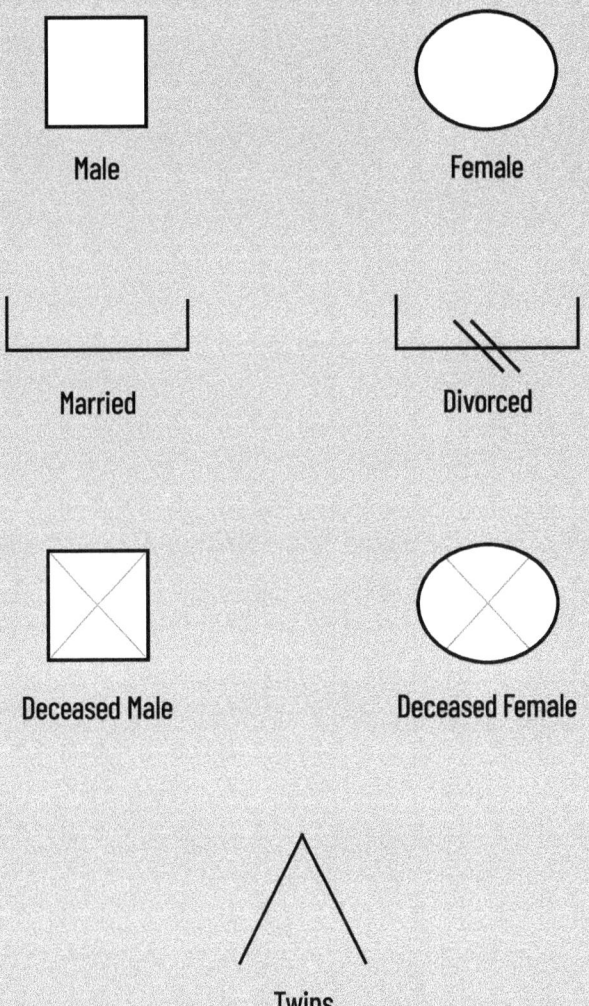

Male

Female

Married

Divorced

Deceased Male

Deceased Female

Twins

Key Players

STELLA
Daddy's Childhood Caretaker / Boorhem Kids' Childhood Caretaker

EARLINE
Daddy and Pat's Housekeeper / Daddy's End-of-Life Caretaker

J.J.
Earline's Cousin / Daddy's "Night Man"

LORENZO
Farm Manager / Horse Whisperer / Late-Night Rescue Squad

JOHN VAN AMBURGH
Daddy's Business Partner / Best Friend / Accomplice

JIMMY
Owner of Main Street Café / Bill Boorhem Worshipper

KOUNTRY KITCHEN
Shreveport Gossip Spot for Daddy and Cronies

MAIN STREET CAFÉ
Only Decent Restaurant in the County / Shrine to Foxwood

VIVIAN TRUCK STOP
Daddy's 2nd Favorite Place to Eat / Home of Toothless Waitress

ZAC THE CAT
Daddy's Cat / Harriet's Nemesis

FOXWOOD PLANTATION
Daddy's Beloved Horse Farm

CRUSHERS, INC
Daddy & John's Business / The "Rock Crusher"

DING DONGS
Harriet's Drug of Choice to Survive Daddy-with-Dementia

FOX NEWS
Daddy's and Ross's Favorite TV Station / Sworn Enemy of Boorhem Sisters

The Why and What For

I'VE CARRIED MY FATHER'S JOURNEY through the debilitating and deadly disease of dementia in my head for almost ten years. As another anniversary of his death approaches, I'm finally ready to tell the story. It is not only a story of the last years of my father's life; it is also the story of the transformation I experienced through walking that walk with him. Though the outcome of such a journey is always tragic, my father's was transformative for me and instrumental, through our caring for him, in bringing my siblings and me much closer together.

At turns hysterically funny, terrifying, and unbearably sad, this journey with him radically changed my life for the better. Our relationship up to that point had been tenuous at best, and non-existent at worst. Fraught with anger, longing, misunderstanding, and constant disapproval, my feelings about him remained conflicted and raw for years. Up to the day I began my turn at taking care of him, I preferred to love him from afar rather than deal with the strings and complications of loving him up close. It was just so much easier.

My siblings never understood my love/hate relationship with my father, nor my perspective about our family. There were so many times I felt as if I'd been dropped into the wrong family, that there were so many better ways to raise kids than how we were raised, and I was totally alone and isolated in my viewpoint.

I distanced myself for years, hotly criticizing our family dynamics and relationships, and I spent years in therapy trying to heal the feelings of abandonment and rejection by, and rage about, my parents that were ever-present. I blamed my siblings for "drinking the Kool-Aid"—except for my older brother, Bill, who was disowned by our father at least once and therefore exempt—and stayed angry at them for years.

But my brother Ross and I stayed connected. Joined at the hip from toddlerhood, I used to say that ours was the only truly reciprocal relationship I ever had. We talked almost every day—he was there for me during my too-many marriages and divorces, and I was there for him when he came out as gay. Because of that closeness, Ross never stopped trying to bring me back into the fold. He is a gatherer of people and was not happy when his tribe was split.

I can't pinpoint exactly when I gave up my anger and resentment and learned to accept my family as they are. I know after my last divorce they were very supportive, which helped *a lot*, and having a darling baby girl that my stepmother Pat could spoil rotten didn't hurt. However, when I paired up with someone they did not like, I was again on the outside looking in, which was mostly my doing, not theirs. Ross and Bill actually liked my partner, and Pat, as always, was totally gracious to him; but the rest of the tribe, especially Daddy (as usual), just couldn't understand why on earth I chose him. But that's a whole 'nother story.

When I came to the realization that I am just not cut out for relationships, I breathed a huge sigh of relief—as did my family, most likely!—and relaxed into my true self. I also relaxed a lot about Daddy and my sibs and decided just to love them, enjoy them, and try to make up for so much lost time.

And I did. I began sharing more of myself with no editing, and guess what? No one freaked out, no one hated me, and I was still standing. Ross and I stayed close, even though we have radically different politics, and I got closer to my sisters. I began to appreciate and like all of them and gained tremendous peace about our family's weirdness, chaos, dysfunctions, and glories. It was nice to be back in the fold, even if it was imperfect, crazy, loud, and raucous.

But enough about me. This is my father's story. Dementia changed my father and how he related to me, mostly for the better. He was softer, more available, kinder—most of the time—and more human. The one thing about him that never changed, however, was his outrageous sense of humor and lightning-quick wit. But as our roles changed, so did my perception of him. He went from "Daddy," and all the baggage attached to that role, to a real person with whom I could actually talk and have a relationship.

During those last years, I felt appreciated and valued by him for the first time in my life. One day around Christmastime, I asked him if Santa brought him anything. After a long pause he said, "Well, he brought me *you!*"

Another time, as we were getting ready for bed, Daddy wanted me to rub lotion on his back. After I finished, I asked him if he felt better, and he said he did. Then I joked, "Thank God for Jergens!"

He laughed, paused a minute, and said, "And thank God for you!"

Those two sentences changed my life. I knew my father loved me, even when he was being a total asshat. But I never really knew if he valued me. I knew then. And it made all the difference.

In therapy-speak, we call these moments *corrective emotional experiences*—times when you experience something that heals a past wound or trauma. I had many of these while caring for Daddy, and for that I am grateful.

Finally, this is the story of our journey together at the end of his life. For me, it was fun, enlightening, exhausting, hilarious, tragic, transformative, and unforgettable. It is also a testimony for family and friends who want to remember the outrageous personality of "Crusher Bill" and for people who want an honest, unfiltered look at a family coping with dementia. Our journey was funny, imperfect, sad, raucous, crazy, and loud; and you can count on a rollicking good time and some tears as you get to know us and my father. Bill Boorhem was larger-than-life, no doubt; to be up close and personal with him in his last days was beyond unforgettable.

———————

MY DADDY-WITH-DEMENTIA WEEKENDS MEANT MANY trips to Belcher, Louisiana, a small town outside of Shreveport. My father bred racehorses and owned a horse farm, Foxwood Plantation, out in the middle of nowhere. He and my stepmother, Pat, built it from the ground up to be the top thoroughbred breeding farm in Louisiana.

For years I got lost trying to find my way out to that farm and then back out to civilization. I called the area "Civil-War-era Belcher" because of how backwoods it seemed to me. The farm, however, was beautiful. I learned to look forward to those trips and used my driving time to catch up on NPR radio shows, talk to my peeps on the phone, daydream, or just be quiet.

I chronicled every trip I made to see Daddy on Facebook. I'm an over-sharer on social media, so it seemed natural to document the hilarity and tragedy of this journey. As I posted, more and more of my friends became Crusher Bill fans. I would alert them when it was time to visit "Civil-War-era Belcher," and they would wait breathlessly for the latest funny quotes, adventures, setbacks, and doings of life with Crusher Bill.

I told Daddy what Facebook was and that he had garnered quite a fan club, and that they loved hearing about our time together. He *loved* that and had a very strong opinion of what to do with the Facebook posts: "Well, hell. You should publish the damn things. It'd make a great book and be a bestseller!"

So, I am, and that is your answer to the question, "Why did Harriet write this book?" Because he wanted me to. I saved the entire journey in Facebook posts, and they are the backbone of this book. It is not a linear account. In fact, it is quite circuitous with chapters written as inspiration hit me about a quote, or an adventure, or a question I asked him. At times, it drags all my brothers and sisters into the mix, along with quite a few ancestors and friends of my father.

It is also chock-full of the Boorhem flair for the cuss word. My father used quite colorful language and, therefore, so do his children. My brother Bill, God rest his soul, could put a string of cuss words together that would blow the Devil's mind. The rest of us are not far behind, with the f-word being one of our favorite expressions; consequently, if you are offended by such language, you should pass this book along right now to someone who doesn't give a flip and is not easily taken aback by outrageous talk.

I hope Daddy was right and that it is a bestseller—only because everyone on earth needs to know William Boorhem, aka Daddy, aka Popio, aka Crusher Bill. Born into the Greatest Generation, he was the epitome of that era: patriotic, self-made, brash, brave, and bigger than life. The men and women of that generation will soon be gone, with only the stories we tell about their time here keeping them alive.

My father, like others of that generation, deserves to be remembered. They really don't make 'em like him anymore. His life was important. His accomplishments many. His impact far and wide. Dementia diminished his present but not his history. It stole his memory from him but not from us; it's our job to make sure that memory lives beyond the confines of dementia, beyond the confines of his death.

Into the Rotation

WHEN I GOT THE CALL from Ross that I needed to get into the rotation of taking care of Daddy, I decided two things: first, I was going to ask him everything I ever wanted to know but was afraid to ask—after all, he had dementia and wouldn't remember—and second, I was going to let him eat and do whatever he wanted whenever he wanted as long as it didn't kill him. Ding Dongs for breakfast? Great. Chase the imaginary cat around the yard? Sure. Cake for dinner? Great idea.

When I got that call, I also had to face the fact that my father, after all, was not immortal and probably didn't have that much time left on earth. If I was ever going to mend our relationship, now was the time. I had to put on my big-girl panties and face my demons. And his.

Thus began what I've christened the Year of Grace: a year of sacred conversations, fabulous stories told and retold, adventures in dining-out-with-Daddy, "Here Kitty, Kitty" stories, and the coming together of my siblings and me for the purpose of serving our father in the best way possible. It was a year of hilarious stories of Daddy-with-dementia, sad and painful stories of Daddy-with-dementia, the creation of the new malady Post-Traumatic Foxwood Disorder, homicidal tendencies toward Daddy, guilt for feeling homicidal, uncontrollable laughter at the crazy happenings, and the need to crawl under the covers and hide from the world for days at a time after leaving the farm.

I wouldn't have traded any of it for the world.

But why call it the Year of Grace? Because grace comes to us unbidden and unmerited from divine goodwill. Part of the Christian definition of grace calls it the divine influence operating in individuals for their regeneration and sanctification. Although I don't call myself a Christian, I like that definition. That year was profoundly regenerating and sanctifying for me.

Daddy probably never knew the impact of that year on me. His dementia, as tragic as it was, gave me the grace and time to mend fences, love him in new ways, dig deep into my inner strength, and care for this man who, in his own way, had cared for me. It was the greatest honor of my life.

Welcome to *The Year of Grace.*

The Beginning

ON THE WAY TO THE farm to see Daddy, I count hawks on fence posts and listen to NPR as I prepare myself to be Helpful Harriet and feel time regress the farther east I head. I jokingly tell my friends I'm headed to Civil-War-era Belcher, and I'm not far wrong.

The road from Shreveport to the farm is cotton on either side for literally miles and miles. Interspersed between the cotton fields are ancient wooden shanties or frame houses with old beat-up

The Foxwood Plantation house, Belcher, Louisiana.

Cotton fields on the way to Foxwood, circa 2012.

Handmade Foxwood Plantation sign made by Ross's friend Barry, pointing the way to the farm, circa 2012.

cars and kitchen appliances in the front yard. Every now and then I see a scraggly horse or cow. When I look at the cotton fields, I half expect to see slaves bent over in the back-breaking work of picking cotton. But I don't. And I don't see any other people. Nowhere in sight. If they are there, they certainly don't show themselves.

At the turn-off to the farm, there is a handmade sign announcing that Foxwood Plantation is down the road. Depending on the time of day, I see all kinds of wildlife—deer, hawks, an owl or two, one coyote, and then, of course, the cows. Daddy always has cows. "Why," I asked one time, "do you always have a farm and cows?"

"Well, shit. I figure if the world ends, I can still grow vegetables and eat the cows."

A strange outlook, since the only things my father ever grew were tomatoes and I can't really see him slaughtering a cow.

Huge live oaks spread their heavy wings to greet me as I turn on the road into the farm. I hear the cows lowing and see huge bales of hay rolled up in every pasture. Green, green, green. It's breathtaking. Crossing the dam, stories of past Fourth of July fireworks fun and mishaps fill my head. The "lake" is fairly low but still calming. Huge crepe myrtle, now in full bloom, line the long driveway up to the house. The farm is absolutely beautiful this time of year. Earline has planted flowers around all the trees, and the huge pecans are fully leafed out, shading everything. I can't see it, but a little farther down the road is the barn with the babies and their mamas. Daddy breeds thoroughbred racehorses, and this time of year is when the new babies arrive.

You haven't lived until you've been in a pasture with a bunch of babies. They bump and jostle you looking for treats, blow steam and snot all over you, crowd so close you think they're gonna crush you. But they don't. They nuzzle and lean against you, rubbing their barn-horse-hay-mama scent all over you. Their fuzzy coats have dirt and grass and slobber from the other babies all over them, and standing up like wire brushes, their baby manes could pass for mohawk haircuts. Every once in a while, one will bolt from the huddle with baby horse zoomies, tearing around the corral bucking and snorting, showing off for the other babies and us. All legs and ears with a short whip of a tail, they are totally full of themselves. And their eyes. I could drown in them. The deepest, wettest brown you've ever seen. I love them so much.

One year, Pat named a baby after every grandchild. Leslie's Love was my youngest daughter's and actually won several races. Leslie was crushed when "her" horse got claimed in a race and was gone; kids have no understanding of adult shenanigans, and it took her—and me, unbeknownst to her—a long time to forgive Popio for that one. After seeing Leslie's heartbreak, Pat never named another baby after the grandkids.

———————

I pull up to the house, park behind Daddy, gird my loins, and enter through the kitchen door.

"Hey, Daddy!"

"What the hell are *you* doing here?" he asks.

"I came to see you, silly."

"Whatever for?"

"Can't I come to the farm just because I want to see you?"

"Well, that's suspect. What do you want?"

"Nothing. Just came to see you."

I wasn't about to tell him that I was on Daddy-with-dementia duty and that it was my turn to be the weekend caretaker. That would have thrilled him to no end, and I'd have been out on my butt or made the butt of a cussing tirade that would have lasted all weekend and made the Devil sign up for Crusher Bill cussing lessons. "Well...hell..."

This goes on every time I show up. Sometimes I think the only one he is really happy to see is my brother Ross, but only because he has Daddy's complete television schedule on his iPhone. The first question out of his mouth is always, "Where's Ross?" And the second is, "When is he coming?"

"He was just here, Daddy. Besides, I'm your favorite child, right?"

"Well, that may be, but *he's* my favorite worker!"

Jesus.

Growing Up Boorhem

In observance of National Family Week, and anticipation of Mothers Day on May 8, we salute the charming Boorhem family who live at 3924 Gillon. Left to right, front row are Harriet, Beth, Barbara and Ross; back row, Mr. William Boorhem, Bill, Ann and Mrs. Boorhem.

Newspaper article in the *Dallas Morning News* celebrating Mother's Day—the perfect family! 1950s.

BEING ONE OF SIX CHILDREN means you are part of a tribe. Our tribe consisted of four girls (Ann, Beth, Barbra, and Harriet) and two boys (Bill and Ross). We were stairstep kids, with only six years between Bill, the oldest, and Ross, the youngest. The unexpected pair of twins—Beth and Barbra—in the middle narrowed the age gap between all of us. Ann was second oldest but really acted like the oldest because Bill was never around, and Ross and I were the youngest, born only fourteen months apart.

The Boorhem Tribe in "The Awkward Years"; love those "flip" hairdos! Top L-R: Bill, Ann, Beth; bottom L-R: Harriet, Mother, Ross, Daddy, Barbra, early- to mid-1960s.

I asked Daddy one time why he and Mother had so many kids and whether they had planned to have six. His reply? "Probably not, but what the hell else was there to do in Malvern, Arkansas?"

Our tribe was extremely lucky to have two gorgeous parents. My father was handsome to the max, and my mother was truly beautiful. All of us came out looking like some combo of the two, and as an old friend of my grandmother's said at the time, "Not an ugly one in the bunch!"

One of the fun things about a big family is the variety of how the genes show up in each kid—how we can look and act so much alike and yet different at the same time. However, there are certain Boorhem traits that manifested in *all* of us.

The Boorhem Chin: My father had a distinctly square chin that every child born into the Boorhem clan after him has in some form or fashion. My siblings and I, our kids, and our kids' kids have all come into the world welcomed by whoever was at their birth by "He/she's got the Boorhem chin!"

The Boorhem Jawline: My father had the classically handsome bone structure that makes women swoon that included his infamous jawline—that movie-star-like strong, squared-off bone that drops straight down from the ear and makes a hard turn right or left into the chin. Add the strength of that formation to his distinctive chin, and you had "The Boorhem Look." Every single one of us has that exact look, thus, "Not an ugly one in the bunch!"

When I was posting pictures of my father on Facebook, one was of him in the cockpit of one of the planes he flew. You could barely see him, but one of my friends posted, "OMG! Even from that distance you can see the 'Boorhem Look!'" She was right—that's how distinctive the "look" is. Consequently, wherever we went together or alone, we never stopped hearing, "Boy, I can tell you're a Boorhem!"

Daddy in his Navy flight gear. He and I look so much alike, it's kinda scary! 1943.

Harriet, 2018. Example of the Boorhem Look: eyes, chin, jawline.

Daddy flying a WWII bomber—the Boorhem Look is evident even from afar!

Daddy's high school senior picture, 1939. He looks just like
Beth to me in this picture—but
the Boorhem Look is definitely there!

Daddy's high school graduation picture,
1939.

Another high school picture. I stay amazed at
how much of him is in all of us! Strong genes!

Daddy, beginnings of the Boorhem Look, date unknown.

Mother with the tribe. Ross is on her lap. On her left side are Bill and Ann, with Harriet in front. On her right is Beth, with Barbra in front.

Daddy with the tribe, Malvern, Arkansas, 1952.

The Boorhem Eyes: Both my parents had blue eyes, and sure enough, we all came out with blue eyes. However, what makes them *Boorhem eyes* is not only the fact that they are blue; it's the shape of our eyes that tells the tale. My father had deep-set almond-shaped eyes, and even though my mother's eyes were fairly deep-set, they were much rounder and larger than my dad's. Daddy's genes won again on that front. If you were to

Mother with the surprise twins, Beth (L) and Barbra (R). They each weighed 7 ½ lbs at birth! Poor Mother, 1949.

take a picture of each of us showing only our eyes and then compare them, you would not be able to tell who was who, except maybe Ann, who got a bit more of Mother's rounded shape than anyone else did.

Height: Here's where things begin to diverge. My father was a slight man, being only 5'10" or 5'11" in his prime. However, my mother's father and his brother were both well over 6' tall, and my mother was 5'8". Half of us (Bill, Ross, and me) got the tall genes, and the other half (Ann, Beth, and Barbra) got either the medium tall or not-so-tall genes. Bill used to be 6'2", and

Daddy looking like a gangster with all of us. Bill and Ann are next to Daddy, then front row, L-R: Barbra, Beth, Harriet, Ross, 1954.

Ross is 6'4". I'm 5'9" and Ann and Beth (before they shrank) were 5'6' to 5'7", with Barbra being the shorty at 5'5". Ross and I are the only ones who haven't shrunk, and I credit years of yoga for keeping me stretched to the max. If my sisters had only listened to me all those years I was trying to get them to do yoga, they too could have stayed their original heights!

Here's what's astonishing to me: as slight a man as my father was, he could scare the pants off of every one of us, including my 6'2" and 6'4" brothers. And when I look through family pictures, I am once again astonished that I was taller than my father for most of my adult life, and he still could scare me half to death. He loomed very large despite his short stature.

Christmas on Gillon Ave. Top row: Bill, Beth, Barbra, Lady, Ann; bottom row: friend Andrea, Harriet, Ross. My mother loved ukuleles, which Beth is playing, late 1950s.

Boorhem Speak: My father cussed like a sailor. He also had his famous Crusher Bill sayings. My mother, on the other hand, never uttered a curse word. The worst I ever heard her say was "damn." She was also a grammar and manners aficionado and expected the same from us. Woe be unto whoever chose to put their elbows on the table or end a sentence with a preposition—Mother would be on you like stink on shit. Consequently, we all acted a bit like Eddie in *Leave it to Beaver*: sickeningly polite and mannerly around our parents and adults, with cuss words ready any other time.

Kids pick up mannerisms and ways of speaking from their parents, and we were no different. Plus, we all sounded exactly alike and could imitate both parents to a tee. Mother's "Oh, Lord" lament was second nature to us and probably should be on my sisters' and my gravestones, we say it so much: "Oh, Lord, she just up and died."

Likewise, my father's "goddamnit," "hell no," "dumbass," and "huh!" all became part of our lexicon early in life—just not around Mother. I was literally cussing full-on by the time I reached third grade. When I had my girls, I had to tell them that I didn't care if they cussed, but other people probably did, so save it for home. "Don't try this at school" was the cue to clean up their language.

Decibel Level: I always feel especially sorry for guests who encounter the Boorhem clan for the first time. Our tagline should be "The Loud Family." Why say something at a normal decibel level when you can blow out everyone's eardrums instead? There is not a quiet one in the bunch. At family gatherings, it's survival of the fittest as to who gets heard and who gets ignored. And woe unto anyone who is cursed by being seated anywhere within twenty miles of us in a restaurant. They might as well pack up and go home because we are going to be there all night being *very* loud.

Dramatic Flair: Boorhems love drama. We speak dramatically, we gesture dramatically, we tell dramatic stories. We *are* drama. My sister Beth added a fake Southern accent to her speech (she would never admit it's fake) some years ago, and it takes everything I have to not bust out laughing when she uses it. We all exaggerate, make mountains out of molehills when telling a story, and love astonishing people with an uncalled-for f-bomb. It's no wonder I loved theater in high school and college—I was surrounded by it my entire life.

Daddy and Beth at who knows where. Probably at a racetrack.

The girls—L-R: Ann, Harriet, Barbra, Beth—in our younger years at Ann's daughter, Andrea's, wedding, circa early 1990s.

Humor: The Boorhem DNA consists of no small measure of humor: funny stories, clever comebacks, hilarious asides, quick wit, dry sarcasm, self-deprecation, and merciless teasing of each other. I blame my father—he handled whatever life threw at him or us with humor, i.e., whenever we would report something bad that happened to us, his first response was *always*, "So besides that, Mrs. Lincoln, how was the play?"

Unless the first thing out of his mouth was "Dumbass!"

He was simply hilarious, and frankly, so are the rest of us.

Christmas at our house on Mockingbird Lane in Dallas. Ann and Bill are in the back row. Front row, L-R: Ross, Barbra, Harriet, Beth, circa late 1950s.

Christmas or Thanksgiving in Dallas. Mother at the head of the table; Nonna, Beth, and Bill on the left side; and Harriet, Barbra, Ann, and Ross on the right side, circa mid-1950s.

Bill and Ann, the leaders of the pack, mid-1950s.

The unexpected twins! Beth (L) and Barbra (R).

Six little butts on a couch. We hardly ever wore shirts—no idea why Barbra is wearing one, and the only reason Ann is, is because she loved that outfit. L-R: Barbra, Beth, Ross, Harriet, Bill, Ann.

Young girls! L-R: Ann, Beth, Barbra, Harriet. We were at Nonna's one summer, and she decided we needed to have a picture done to commemorate our stay with her, circa early 1960s.

Mother and the girls on some Easter. L-R: Beth, Barbra, Mother, Ann, Harriet. Mother was huge on holiday pictures. Looking like the perfect family, circa 1964.

Pointy boobs! What happened to Harriet's? I call these pictures "The Awkward Years." L-R: Harriet, Barbra, Ann, Beth, 1964–65.

Here we are again, this time with Daddy. The pointy boobs are not quite as noticeable, and the girls are joined by Daddy, Bill, and Ross, 1963–64.

Ross and Bill at Easter, mid-1960s. Notice the window behind Ross on the porch. Beth and I used to sneak out of that window all the time and invite boys in through that window. We thought it was all unbeknownst to our parents, until one day we came home from school and found every bedroom window nailed shut. Mother never said a word!

Another Easter picture. Notice the hats and gloves! Also notice the "Boorhem chin" on all of us, early 1960s.

Mother and Daddy at Easter. Just another example of our gorgeous parents, early 1960s.

Yet another Easter picture, circa early 1960s.

This photo is hilarious to me because Ann and Bill look like an old married couple with their children! Notice Ross's flattop, which was kept in place with some kind of pink gel—I'm surprised his hair didn't turn pink.

Bill and Ross at Easter at the Gillon Avenue house in Dallas. Looking at Ross in this picture, I'm surprised he grew up to be 6'4"!

Mother and the tribe—probably some Easter. Back row: Ann and Bill. Front row, L-R: Barbra, Beth, Ross, Harriet. Notice Ross is looking the wrong way—not unusual. Also notice the Boorhem chin on everyone.

Mother, half of the beautiful gene pool, early 1950s.

Mother and Daddy when they lived in Atlanta, circa mid-1970s.

ON THE FLIP SIDE, MY father was terrifying and mean as hell. His favorite pet name for most people, including his children, was "Dumbass." If you missed the honor of being called this by him at least once, you just weren't around him much.

My favorite "Dumbass" story happened to me the night of my sixteenth birthday party. I had invited my six best girlfriends to spend the night and go "bombing around town" in my brand-new used 1966 Chevy Impala. We were all in high spirits as we crammed into the car—three in the front and four in the back, illegally, by the way—and took off down Hopson Street to go find friends on the Drag. My birthday is in January, so it was pitch dark at 6:00 p.m., but we didn't care. Off we flew down to the corner, turned right onto Birch Street, and gunned it a block to Woods Street at which point I decided I needed to light a cigarette. This was back in the old days when cars had those cigarette lighters in them that you pushed in and then held to the tip of your cigarette to light when the coil was hot. Still gunning it, I bent down to put the lighter to my cig while tearing left at the corner of Woods and Birch.

BAM! CRASH! CRUNCH!

WTF?

Looking up, I saw that I had failed to notice a *parked car* sitting in front of the corner house at Woods and Birch and had run smack dab into it! Front-ending my brand-new car.

"Shit, shit, shit...I am toast! Oh my god, my dad is going to *kill* me. Shit, shit, shit, SHIT!"

Finally remembering I wasn't the only one in the car, I turned around, assessed the damage, and asked, "Y'all OK?"

Cynthia, who was next to me in the front, had a good gash right below her knee, but everyone else was OK.

"Hell no, we're not OK! Didn't you see that stupid car?"

"No! Did y'all? Why didn't you yell or something?"

"We didn't see it either. It's *black*!"

About that time, the owners of the house came out to see

what all the noise was about, saw their car, looked at us, and much nicer than we deserved, asked, "Y'all all right?"

"Yessir. I'm *so* sorry—I couldn't see your car—it's black!"

"Well, we need to call your parents."

The rest of that night is a total blank, except for the part where I vividly remember my father driving up beside my car, getting out, looking at me, looking at my terrified friends, looking at the car, and looking at the owner of the car. He didn't say something comforting or ask if we were all right.

Instead, he roared, "DUMBASS!"

MY LEAST FAVORITE TIME I was called "Dumbass" was when Ross was in treatment for cocaine addiction. Having snorted the five hamburger restaurants he owned up his nose and having lost everything, he decided it was time to get clean or die.

I don't know how much you know about treatment centers, but they have this thing called Family Week, where you spend a week learning all about addiction and the twelve-step program while participating in group and family therapy with the addict. Of course, I went, and miracle of miracles, Daddy also went and behaved quite well, except on one occasion.

We were involved in this stupid ropes course where we had to figure out some problem with a partner involving ropes, beams, and various other paraphernalia. If we did it faster than the other folks in the game, we would win a prize. Ross was in a therapy group, so Daddy was my partner. That is your first clue to what came next.

While trying to untangle some rope that we were supposed to then wrap around ourselves in a very awkward fashion, I got confused and couldn't figure out how to untie one knot. We were in a gym, which, as you know, is a space prone to very loud echoes, and Daddy, while watching me, bellowed, "Dumbass! Let me do it!" loud enough to be heard in the next county.

Ann and Daddy at the farm in Bells. She was always his favorite. Notice she full-on has the Boorhem Look, circa early 1970s.

Ann and Daddy at the farm in Bells, 1970s. Notice that Ann is almost as tall as Daddy. She out-grows him quickly!

The guys at the farm in Bells. Back row: O.E. (Beth's husband), Daddy, Bill; front row: Ross, Don (Ann's husband). When they weren't playing Risk in the trailer, they were raising hell in other ways, mid-1970s.

The eyes have it! Silly pic of the sibs at some Christmas. L-R: Harriet, Ross, Ann, Beth, Barbra, circa 2016.

Everyone stopped dead in their tracks and turned to stare at us. An eerie silence fell over the gym while they tried to decide how to respond to such an untherapeutic outburst in such a supposedly therapeutic setting.

I could have murdered my father on the spot. It was a good thing I was not holding a gun because Bill Boorhem would have been deader than a doornail quicker than you could say "What the fuck just happened?" I felt the heat rise in me as embarrassment, rage, confusion, and fear took hold. Every terrifying and enraging incident I had ever experienced with him came flooding back, paralyzing my entire body—I completely dissociated. Frozen to the spot, all I was aware of was the incredible heat in my face and my extraordinarily strong urge to kill my father. Somehow, though, I swam back to the surface through all that shame and rage and got up the gumption to bellow back, "I am not a dumbass! Do not ever call me that again!"

"Then untie the damn knot—we're gonna lose the game!"

"I could not care less about losing this stupid game. I repeat: I am not a dumbass! Never use that word again when referring to me!"

Dead silence.

"Well, hell…"

I got no apology, but he did nicely help me untie the knot, and we went on our not-so-merry way. Meanwhile, everyone else pretended like nothing at all had occurred (probably just like they did with their own families), and the infernal ropes course came to an end.

I can't say that was a corrective emotional experience. I would instead call it one of those Fucking Growth Experiences. As painful as it was, however, it seemed to put Daddy on notice that I was not a wimp. He never again called me "dumbass," and he behaved like a human being for the remainder of the week. In fact, he was such a gentleman that when Ross came out and told him he was gay, all Daddy said was, "Well, hell. I knew that."

Ross and Harriet at Ross's first Black Tie Dinner, a fundraising event for an AIDS cure, 1996.

"What? How long have you known? Why didn't you ever say anything to me?" Ross asked.

"Oh, I've known a long time. Do you think I'm stupid? But that was your story to tell—not mine," Daddy replied.

Ross, all these many years later, is still flabbergasted by Daddy's response.

"I was so terrified to tell him—everyone else in the entire world knew—everyone but him, or so I thought—and he knew all along. Jesus. What a waste of energy, hiding it all those years."

―――――――――

DADDY'S SLIGHT STATURE BELIED HIS huge presence—he would walk into a room and own it, look you straight in the eye, shake your hand, and bellow, "Hi...Bill Boorhem!" Lord, he was loud. We would all cringe with embarrassment, but everyone loved him—his jokes, his fabulous blue eyes, his larger-than-life personality.

Bill Boorhem never met a stranger. He attributed this to traveling up and down the Mississippi River with his civil engineer father in the 1930s, building bridges and roads for FDR. He attended more schools than he could remember before graduating from high school, saying you had to get to know kids fast—who were the bullies and who was OK. I asked him one time what the worst thing was about attending so many schools, and he retorted, "Having to fight my way into every goddamn one of them." He was tough and popular wherever he went—once he beat up the bullies.

Back to his being mean as hell. He was mean as hell—at least to his children. He went at my older brother more times than I can count with every cuss word known to humans and was not above resorting to violence to get his point across. Brother Bill was mean as hell too, and fought back, so the ruckus was always high volume when they were locked in battle. I watched him take a belt to Barbra and my younger brother, Ross, at different times and was traumatized for years. He never touched me, which caused its own problems—years of survivor guilt and therapy. I learned quickly living with him that the key to survival was to become invisible and quietly do my own thing.

But Lord have mercy, he was fun! Some of my very best memories are of Daddy and the pool, Daddy and the lake, Daddy and the ski boat, Daddy on ski trips, Daddy everywhere. Every Sunday after church when we were little, we would lie down for a nap before going to the pool, and I would lie beside Daddy on the "divan." It was pure heaven. He would play "crocodile" with us in the pool and throw us all over the place. He taught us how to dive, how to water ski, how to snow ski. There are so, so many stories of the fun and terror we had with him.

Like the time we were all at the dinner tables—there were so many of us, we had two tables—and Daddy asked Ross to pass the butter. Well, we always had this funny saying: "Lob or bullet?" So Ross asked, "Lob or bullet?"

And Daddy said, "BULLET!"

Ross *threw* the butter dish with butter in it from one side of the kitchen to the other, barely missing Mother. Ross was not able to finish his dinner with us. Notice, however, that Daddy was not held responsible at all.

Or the adventures with the many boats owned by Daddy and John Van Amburgh, each one named *The Jody/Jane* after our mothers. I'm not sure I would have been happy about that if I were them because one caught fire, one bit the dust due to dry rot, I think John probably sank two of them by forgetting to put the drain plug back in, and I know for sure that Daddy ran at least one of them over tree stumps in Lake Catherine or Lake Dallas.

Speaking of which, skiing behind the boat with Daddy at the helm could be a truly harrowing experience. First, you could not get back in the boat till you got up on skis. Second, you had to listen to his incessant, "Keep your butt down! Let the boat pull you up!" Third, you *always* had to be on guard that if you went outside the wake, he would turn the boat in toward you, making the rope slack and then catapulting you in the air when the boat straightened out. Last, if and when you did venture outside the wake, you had better be ready to end up going sixty miles an hour as Daddy gunned the motor in a turn that sent you flying out far to the side—I remember one time turning at least three cartwheels on top of the water before landing flat on my back after falling in one of those turns. And then, of course, he would turn in toward you. Fun, fun. It's a miracle any of us lived.

And then there were the ski trips. One I'm thinking of in particular was especially fun with all of us piled into an antique RV driving up to Taos in a whiteout snowstorm. The fact that we did not drive off that mountain is purely a miracle. We literally

Mother hamming it up at
Lake Catherine, mid-1950s.

Mother looking glamor-
ous in one of the *The Jody/
Jane* boats. I think this was
our first inboard motor,
1955–56.

Water Babies! Fun at Lake Catherine or Lake Bridgeport. L-R: Harriet, Barbra, Beth, Ann, Bill, Ross, 1955–56.

Mother and her brood with one of the many *The Jody/ Jane* boats, circa 1955.

Mother again looking glamorous in one of the *The Jody/Jane* boats. Probably in Arkansas at Lake Catherine, late 1950s.

Daddy retrieving a ski after one of his famous ski lessons, Lake Catherine, late 1950s.

Mother and Daddy, Lake Catherine, Arkansas, late 1950s. I love this photo.

could not see a foot in front of us. That was also the year that Ann almost skied off the mountain, Ross got the nickname "The Yellow Peril" (he had on a yellow jumpsuit that made him look like the Abominable Snow Man), and I got blamed for the crummy skiing conditions because I had planned the trip.

The first ski trip we ever took was to Breckinridge, Colorado, and talk about bad skiing conditions! We were basically in a blizzard the entire time but still skied because, well, that's what you do when you have only four days to be there. None of us had correct ski apparel, and so Scotch-guarded jeans and twenty layers of clothing served as our snow suits. Bad mistake. I ended up sobbing in the ski lodge after a morning lesson of "crow's-footing" up the fucking mountain, soaking wet and freezing my ass off. Even though the fam labeled me "wuss of the year," I did not darken those horrible slopes again.

On other trips when all of us were involved, we often took two cars, and my anxiety level was through the roof the entire time. In the first place, Daddy was, of course, the lead car, and *no one* could keep up with him. In the second place, Barbra was *always* on the floorboard terrified that we would drive off some mountain road going eighty mph—not far from the truth. Oh, and getting carsick—speaking of which, there was the time we were driving to Malvern late at night. The car had no AC, so we drove when it was cooler, and we *all* got sick to the tune of Bill hanging his head out of the station wagon, puking his guts out.

It was always a toss-up which car you wanted to be in—did you want to die with Daddy driving off the mountain or from inhaling secondhand smoke while Mother madly smoked to assuage her terror? Or did you want to die listening to Bill cuss Daddy to the moon and back while running red lights, passing in no-passing zones, and speeding like crazy just to keep up?

Along with trips with my father, his birthday parties were always full of surprises. There was the infamous Sixtieth Birthday Bash at the pool in Farmers Branch at which Ross, in all his great wisdom, thought it would be perfectly appropriate to invite a stripper, with a gazillion underage kids in the pool. In marched the stripper, decked out in red, white, and blue, before beginning to take it all off! Andrea, always the mothering cousin, was mortified and kept trying to cover up Cousin Sarah's eyes, I'm sure unsuccessfully. I don't think any of us knew what was happening and so were in shock; we were just kind of stuck in place! I don't even remember seeing Pat—she may have fled the scene—and I have no recollection of how it ended. What I'm sure of, however, is that Daddy had a good time.

And then there was the infamous Seventieth Birthday Celebration at which I thought it appropriate to dye my hair bright red, wear a very short and low-cut sparkly blue dress, and sing Daddy's favorite big band tunes to him and the crowd. What. Was. I. Thinking? In the one picture I have of Daddy and me standing up in front, he looks rather mortified. Barbra did join me at the end to help, but she looked better than I did, so that just made things worse!

These and so many other hilarious and terrifying stories are so burned into my brain, it would take way longer than the time I have left on this earth to tell them.

However, lest you get lulled into thinking my father was all fun and games, let me remind you that Bill Boorhem was a tough cookie to live with. He could be rigid, closed-minded, obnoxious, angry, loud, and terrifying. Remember, he and Brother Bill went at it so many times, I'm surprised they didn't kill each other, and because Barbra was the second-in-command-rebel, she was not immune to his wrath either. Although Ann was mostly perfect, Beth and I snuck around behind his back and did most everything we wanted, and Ross was mostly missing, all of us at one time or another faced his wrath, his freezeouts, his rants, being grounded for weeks at a time, being "disowned" (Bill and me), and being obliged to beg him for money. He expected nothing but the best, was furious if we made less than straight A's, and was generally uncompromising on most issues.

He was such a conundrum. He absolutely loved music and dancing, taught all of us girls how to ballroom dance, took my sister Barbra and me to many Broadway musicals, was *totally* engaged in life, insatiably curious, a softie if you approached him just the right way (he could *never* say no to Beth—what was *that* about?), a fantastic story and joke teller—even if most of them were totally inappropriate—and a good soul. He bailed more folks out of jail than I can count, helped finance school for many an employee's children, loaned all of us money at one time or another, and I don't know about the rest of my sibs, but most of it I never paid back!

Mother and Daddy in front of our house on Hopson St. in Sherman. Notice she's about as tall as he, late 1960s or early 1970s.

Mother and Daddy with the grandkids; he was always nicer to them than he was to us! Mid- to late-1970s.

Daddy with granddaughter Andrea at the farm in Bells. He loved babies—kids and adolescents, not so much.

Daddy and Mother with Andrea. They were gorgeous parents, mid-1970s.

More Daddy with the grandkids, joined by Ross in this picture, early to mid-1970s.

Daddy and the guys in front of the Hopson Street house. Rodney (Don's brother), Don, O.E., Bill, Daddy, Ross. Ross is now taller than all of them, mid-1970s.

Mother and Daddy with Andi and Becca (Ann's girls) at the farm in Bells. Sadly, my kids never got to meet my mother. She died when I was four months pregnant with Kat, my oldest.

Simply put, he was *always* bigger than life. Never sick even one day. I had just about convinced myself that he might miraculously be immortal—that he *could* be the one to beat the odds. When he was sixty, seventy, eighty, he and Pat ran circles around us. They were constantly on the go to watch their horses run—Shreveport, New Orleans, Hot Springs, Dallas, even California—we never knew where they were or when they were coming back, and honestly, that's how I liked it. Being related to Crusher Bill from afar was much easier than being related from a-close.

Photograph of the young adult Boorhems that we had done for our parents one Christmas. L-R: Ann, Ross, Beth, Barbra, Bill, then I'm at the bottom. Not an ugly one in the bunch! 1970s.

Daddy and Pat at Christmas. He had entered his "chubby" years! Always the ham.

Now It Was Our Turn

THOSE CIRCLES THAT DADDY AND Pat ran around all of us came to a screeching halt when Pat died suddenly and totally unexpectedly.

"She sat right there in that goddamn chair and died" was what Daddy said. He wasn't there—he had been out running errands—and when he got home, he actually walked right past her thinking she was asleep. She wasn't. He tried CPR, but it was too late.

When Ross called me with the news, every ounce of breath was sucked out of me. All I could think about was how in the hell I was going to tell Leslie, my youngest. She idolized Pat, and Pat had spoiled her rotten from the day she was born. Since my mother died before Les was born, Pat was the only grandmother Leslie had on my side of the family. It was going to knock her flat.

It did. It knocked us all flat, especially Daddy. No clue that she had any kind of health problems, none of us were ready for the way she was just suddenly *gone*. Feeling unwell that morning, she told Daddy she was going to take a nap while he went to town, and she never woke up.

Kevin, her son, was, of course, devastated—is still devastated. Pat never got to see him marry Lyndsey, never got to meet her granddaughter Landry, never got to spoil her rotten like she did Leslie, never got to see Kevin's accomplishments as an educator.

I was showing Daddy pictures of everyone one weekend, and when I showed him Landry and told him who she was, he looked at her a long time and said, "I can't believe Pat isn't here to see this baby. She would have been so happy to know her."

Life can really suck.

———————

ANN, BEING THE ONLY ONE who wasn't working full time, got voted to be the stand-in Pat at the farm and to help Daddy with the business side of horse breeding and racing. For five years, she was over in Civil-War-era Belcher two or three days a week with Earline, Daddy's housekeeper and the main caretaker dealing with Crusher Bill. She will undoubtedly sit at the right hand of God for that.

The first two years after Pat's death were spent changing all the legal work they had set up. Daddy was supposed to die first, and since he didn't, *everything* had to be redone. Ann and Daddy navigated lawyers, trust experts, accountants, and bankers—the blind leading the blind. When Pat died, Daddy didn't even know where his checkbook was. At the funeral home, when it came time to pay, he said, "Well shit, I have plenty of money, I just have no goddamn idea where it is or how to get to it." Pat did all that—Pat did everything.

She also hid a lot of things about Daddy from us—mainly, that he was more and more forgetful and was more and more difficult to deal with. Dementia had begun to take hold, we now think, several years before Pat died, but she covered much of it and handled him herself.

Now it was our turn.

———————

I CAME IN AT THE tail end of helping Daddy-with-dementia. Ann and Ross had carried the lion's share of the load after Pat died. They were fried, Ann especially. Both were in their fourth year of caring for Daddy.

Why was I not there earlier? Oh, various excuses: a full-time, all-consuming job; heavy involvement with my youngest in her senior year at the University of Texas; and the fact that no one had asked. The real reason, however, was much more complicated. My father and I had been at odds for years—not estranged—but certainly strained.

It was just easier to stay away.

———————

SINCE DADDY COULDN'T BE ALONE at night, during the week J.J. was Daddy's "night man." A cousin of Earline's, he is huge, affable, and patient as hell. Daddy always had some conspiracy theory going about him—either he was Chinese and here illegally (J.J. is Black), or he was "after" me and I better watch out. Other times he was sure J.J. was stealing him blind or involved in some crime ring. The possibilities were endless and quite entertaining. Every time I came, I had to hear the latest theory. I listened, acted concerned, tried not to bust out laughing, and carried on.

When J.J. first started staying the night, Daddy asked Ann who the *hell* he was and *why* he was staying there. Ann told him that J.J. had been thrown out of his house by his girlfriend and needed a place to stay. Who knows if that was true or if Ann, like me, was trying to circumvent the subject of Daddy needing a caretaker twenty-four hours a day. I'm sure she was even less thrilled than I was at the prospect of a weekend-long cussing tirade about "leave me the hell alone—I'm perfectly fine." At any rate, Daddy evidently bought the story but told Ann in no uncertain terms, "You better as hell be collecting rent from that SOB!"

Later on in the saga of Daddy-with-dementia, Popio called Beth one night and told her she needed to fire J.J. since Ann wouldn't. Who knows what egregious wrong he had committed this time, but Daddy knew he wouldn't get anywhere with Ann, so he went down the list to Beth. A long conversation ensued, and boy am I glad I was not part of that tête-à-tête!

BTW, J.J. was with Daddy until the end. Poor guy, he's probably been in therapy ever since with Post-Traumatic Crusher Bill Syndrome.

———————

The "shrine" to Foxwood Plantation at Main St. Café in Gilliam created by the owner, Jimmy; he idolized my father, circa 2012.

MY BIGGEST FEAR RIGHT NOW is getting lost driving Daddy around. I've not been over here that much, and I have to get directions every time I come. And Daddy is not one to stay home. He has to "go into town" almost every morning to have breakfast with his racing cronies and loves to go to Gilliam or Vivian for dinner. There is a little restaurant called Main Street Café in Gilliam that is a literal shrine to my father. The owner holds my dad in such high esteem that one entire corner of the café is dedicated to pictures, newspaper articles, trophies, and memorabilia about Foxwood Plantation and Daddy's horses. When Zarb's Magic won the Arkansas Derby and went on to the Kentucky Derby back in the day, the entire town of Gilliam was celebrating. Jimmy, the owner, truly loves Daddy.

We're not going anywhere tonight, but tomorrow is "go to town" day. I'm worried. Thankfully, since this is the first

Kentucky Derby, 1996. L-R: Unknown, Pat, Barbra, Daddy, Harriet, Ann, Don, Ann's husband.

Daddy and Pat at a Kentucky Derby party, 1996. No doubt he's saying something totally inappropriate to her.

Daddy dancing with my Aunt Ann at a Kentucky Derby party, 1996.

Daddy's friend, Jim Clark; Ross; Daddy; and Beth at a Kentucky Derby party.

Harriet and Pat at one of the Kentucky Derby parties, May 1996.

Daddy and Harriet at a Kentucky Derby party—Daddy's chubby years! May 1996.

weekend I'm here, Ann is staying tonight to make sure all goes well. I'll get directions from her and hopefully won't end up in bum-fuck-nowhere with Crusher Bill bitching about my driving and my miserable sense of direction.

Things start off fine and then go to hell in a handbasket in less time than it takes to wonder what the fuck happened. A storm blows in. Now, I'm not too worried about storms, and neither is Ann, but this one is a doozy. Thunder, lightning, wind, and rain blowing sideways as it can only in East Texas and Louisiana. And then, of course, the power goes out.

This is when shit hits the fan. Ann gets all tied up in knots saying we can't stay without electricity (I'm not sure why this is such a big deal) and decides she has to figure out how to turn on the generator, which I'm not sure has *ever* been used. The switch is supposed to be on the garage wall, so out we all traipse to investigate, at which time Ann and Daddy immediately get in a screaming match about how to turn on the fucking generator.

Daddy starts: "Goddammit, let me do it. I know where the switch is."

"No, you don't, and you can't see shit!"

"Hey! This is *my* house, and I'm in goddamn charge here!"

"Not right now, you're not, so get out of my way so I can get this damn thing started!"

I'm sure it is excruciating, ceding his power to a girl child; so of course her telling him that he is not in charge pisses him off even more, and they continue fighting and arguing over the generator switch for quite some time. Finally, Ann finds the damn switch, and the fucking generator struggles to life—voila! We have electricity.

I'm not sure all that was worth it. I might have rather sat in the dark all night than witnessed that battle.

But witnessing battles seemed to be my role in the family. I was rarely in them, usually just watching or listening to them, which had its own consequences for my psyche. My first memory of such observation was when I was four years old. I was sitting on the kitchen floor (why?) watching my mother and one of my sibs locked in some kind of parent-child argument—except that you *did not* argue with my mother, so my sib was losing badly. I distinctly remember saying to myself—at age four—"This could be done so much better than that!"

The theme of my life. It explains so much: the reason I became a therapist, my too-many marriages, my radical feminist anger, the way I parented my girls, the kind of leader I became. I always thought there was a better way to be, do, act, love, lead, help. It shaped everything I was and did, for better or worse.

The worst battle I ever witnessed was between my brother Bill and Daddy. Bill had been estranged from the family for several years because of his long hair, "radical" political views, love of Bob Dylan and all resistance music, penchant for various drugs, and involvement with the SDS—Students for a Democratic Society—a left-wing "anarchist" group.

I hadn't seen him in several years when late one night I heard this tap, tap, tap on my window—my bedroom opened out onto the front porch. I looked out, and there was Bill, with all his glorious long hair and guitar in hand, saying, "Let me in!"

Shit, shit, shit! Boy did I wish right about then that I was anywhere on earth or outer space but in that bedroom or that fucking house. I knew right then that WWIII was about to erupt, but loyal sister that I was, I let him in, and he snuck down to the basement—the "boy's room"—for the night.

According to Beth, Mother had stayed in touch with Bill the entire time he was disowned, so she may have known that he was coming into town. Of course, no one else knew, especially not Crusher Bill.

Our grandmother Hattye happened to be staying with us at that time, and she, along with Beth, Barbra, Bill's girlfriend Donna, and I got to witness the melee that quickly followed when Daddy discovered Bill's appearance. We were huddled in the girls' bathroom (it was very large) smoking cigarettes—yes, all of us except Ann smoked in our teens—and talking about anything but what was actually happening. I have no idea where Ross was—probably hiding in the basement with Lady, the dog.

Mother, meanwhile, was in the kitchen wiping counters (her anxiety reliever) while Daddy and Bill went at it. Loud enough for all the neighbors to hear, they argued and fought, fought and argued, the battle roiling out onto the driveway and ending with them yelling obscenities at each other, neither one willing to give an inch even if hell froze over.

Who knows what they were arguing about or what they even actually said? There was so much rage, disappointment, judgment, and just plain shit flying back and forth that it was hard to tell. All I know is that we didn't see Bill for years after that battle. I don't even know when or how Donna left the scene of the chaos—or where or how they went.

What a complete and total shit show that, by the way, was *never talked about again*. Not a word from Mother, nada from Daddy, and even us kids didn't talk about it amongst ourselves until many years later. It was as if it had never happened; we just didn't see Bill again for a very long time. Even Hattye played the game of "everything is fine" once it was over.

It's not surprising that Mother never uttered a word about it. She was a total and complete stoic. How she went through life showing *no one* her feelings is beyond me. I'll never forget a letter I wrote to her once telling her I wanted to be closer and get to know her better. Her response was, "I bare my soul to no one but God."

You know, though, back then nobody in our world talked about anything! It was the late '60s, the Vietnam War was in full swing, and protests were happening all over the US, but none of that existed in Sherman, Texas. It just wasn't discussed. All those nice Southern families just put on their happy faces. When Kent State happened, I was in French class at Grayson County Jr.

Brother Bill, 1946–2002. He was always in trouble with Daddy. We lost him way too early at the young age of fifty-six to idiopathic pulmonary fibrosis—cause completely unknown. Miss you, Bro.

Bill after he cleaned up his hippie act and became an "oil baron," date unknown.

Our house on Hopson Street in Sherman. If those walls could only talk! They heard every word of every battle.

College, and my French teacher came in crying. None of us could figure out why—we were so disconnected from the real world.

Oh, shit happened, don't get me wrong. Just like everywhere else in the world where there are people, bad stuff followed. We had alcoholics and crazy folks, affairs and suicides, untimely deaths and terrible illnesses. Teenagers died in car wrecks, young men were sent off to war, and women cleaned up their husbands' messes. We were no different from any other town—we just didn't talk about it.

Nothing was ever said about anything—what the fuck we talked about is anyone's guess, but we certainly *did not* talk about anything real.

No wonder I spent years in therapy.

———

DADDY: "WE GOING INTO TOWN in the morning?"

    Me: "Sure. What time do you want to go?"

    Daddy: "Oh, whenever I get up."

Me: "Uh, well, that could be pretty late. How about I wake you up about 8:30?"

Daddy: "Well, shit. OK. Guess I'd better go to bed then. Do we have any cake?"

Me: "No, but we have Ding Dongs." Remember, I said he could eat whatever he wanted!

Daddy: "How about a few of those with some coffee?"

My father never stopped drinking real coffee, even late at night. It never kept him awake—he drank it all day and all night, the stronger the better, and always black.

We were sitting at the table one time. It was toward the end of the dementia progression: Daddy had deteriorated, couldn't process his words very well, and had a hard time communicating. As we sat there talking, Daddy moved his hand slowly up to his mouth and back down to the table time and time again as if he were drinking a cup of coffee. *There was no cup of coffee* except in his mind. I never said a word about it—just kept talking.

———————

IT'S SATURDAY MORNING. I WAKE Daddy up at 8:30 to go into town. He's pretty cheerful and alert as he gets ready. I go in to check on him and notice he's got on his boxers, his shorty pajama bottoms over his boxers, and his long pajama bottoms over his shorty pajama bottoms, and he is getting ready to pull on trousers over all of that. "Uh, Daddy, why do you have on three pairs of pants?" I ask.

"What the hell's wrong with three pairs of pants?"

"Nothing…except when you put on your trousers, you'll have on *four* pairs of pants," I explain patiently.

"And? It might be chilly outside."

It's not.

I start to retort with something logical but pause and think better of it, then respond, "Never mind. Just let me know when you're ready."

Daddy and I at his favorite haunt, Kountry Kitchen. I'm showing him how to take an iPhone Selfie. I tried to get a smile out of him, but he chose the grump look, 2012.

Pick your battles. If he goes out looking like the Pillsbury Dough Boy, who gives a shit?

Meanwhile, as I'm choosing which battles to fight, Ross calls to check in: "Hey, Sis. How's it going?"

"He's done pretty well this weekend. Seems pretty perky and with it. He did, however, call you Rodney. Wanted to know when Rodney was coming back."

"Rodney? Where in the hell did he get *that*?" Ross asks.

"No idea," I reply.

"Well, I'll be there next weekend...with my name tag on!"

Daddy isn't the only clever one in the bunch.

So, we get to town without incident or me getting lost—glory be!—and go to his favorite haunt, Kountry Kitchen. Sitting at the table with several of his horse-trainer buddies, we have a very nice breakfast, lots of laughs, and *lots* of coffee. When one of his friends gets up to leave, Daddy leans over to me and whispers conspiratorially, "Who the hell was *that* guy?"

Shocked, I respond, "Daddy, that's Sam, one of your trainers."

Daddy says, "Nah! Never set eyes on that son-of-a-bitch before in my life. He just wanted a free breakfast!"

Lord have mercy.

After Daddy disavows knowing Sam, he's ready to go. And when he's ready, *everyone* better be ready. We get up, and as we're leaving, he asks, "Did we pay the bill?"

"Yeah, I took care of it," I explain.

"Well, you didn't have to do that!"

"Thanks, but I used *your* credit card!" I tell him. Clever retorts seem to be a family trait.

"Well, I'll be goddamned."

Walking to the car, I notice he is coming over to my side. "Daddy, you're getting in the wrong side of the car. You have to get in on the other side."

"I know that! I'm trying to open the goddamn door so you can get your ass inside!"

By this time, I am in dire need of a nap. We get back to the farm, and I announce, "I'm taking a nap. You've worn me out, so do not disturb me unless you are dying."

"OK. I think I'll take one, too."

Thank. You. God.

"Have a nice nap!" I tell Daddy.

"I've never had a bad nap."

———

NAPS ARE A BOORHEM THING. Built into our DNA and passed down through generations, there is nothing we love better than a good nap. Pat used to say that if she walked into a room and everyone was conked out on the couch or the floor, she knew she was in a room full of Boorhems. We are masters of the art. Sunday afternoon naps, Daddy-after-work-and-before-dinner naps, before- and after-swimming naps, holiday-food-coma-naps, no-reason naps. There's nothing better. The world can be shit, but take a nap, and all is new and better again.

My sister Barbra takes a nap *every day* from 3–5 pm, and woe to anyone who interrupts it or keeps it from happening. I myself love nothing better than to walk the dogs early in the morning, come back and take a shower, drink some coconut water, eat a protein bar, and take a short nap with my dogs on the bed. It's a new world afterward! I have even been known to take two naps in one day. Sister Ann swears she can no longer nap, but I don't believe her—she's no longer a Boorhem if that is true.

All Boorhems know a nap is an excellent reason to cut a telephone call short, not answer the phone—actually, we don't need any reason to not answer the phone—delay getting together, ignore the doorbell, or pull down the shades and hide. With all the research on how good naps are for our health, I'm convinced we will all live to be at least a hundred.

———

I'M ON THE COUCH NAPPING, and Daddy is in his chair napping. All is right with the world, especially since I convinced him to turn off Fox Effing News.

Where's the Damn Klonopin?

To say my father and I had a complicated relationship is an understatement. At times I idolized him, was terrified of him, hated him, was so angry with how he treated my siblings and me, was mortified at his uncensored opinions of *everything* and *everybody*, and desperately wanted his approval and for him to be proud of me.

But for now, all of that is far away as we sit on the screen porch drinking in the morning. Mist is rising from the pastures, a cool breeze is beginning to take shape, baby calves are bawling for their mamas, squirrels are skittering up and down the huge pecan trees, and Foxwood Plantation is in fine form.

Screen porches are another family tradition—are actual necessities if you want to sit outside without the millions of mosquitoes and other bugs so prevalent in the South, biting you on every uncovered inch of your skin.

My grandmother Hattye had a stellar screen porch with old wicker chairs and couches with well-worn cushions, metal garden tables, a tongue-in-groove wooden floor and ceiling, and huge hydrangeas blooming all around it. When we visited her with all my cousins, she, my mother, and my Aunt Ann would sit on that porch for hours working on crossword puzzles, smoking cigarettes, telling stories, and gossiping about the goings-on of Malvern, Arkansas. It was on that porch listening to their descriptions of the world and all they loved about it that I acquired my love of old houses, china and crystal, all kinds of flowers, crossword puzzles, gossip, quirky people, and, of course, screen porches. Stories of the blind man with the seeing-eye dog, the old one-legged guy with the mule and cart rumbling around town, Miller's Pharmacy, free cold drinks at Shyrock's, the Ritz Movie Theater, and our adventures at Lake Catherine—all talked and laughed about, dissected, and ruminated on in the confines of that little porch—stay with me till this day.

Daddy is fairly quiet this morning. He hasn't mentioned going into town, which probably means he's tired or doesn't remember that he goes into town every morning. That's fine with me. I would love a quiet day with no drama.

Mother with her mother—Hattye to us, 1950s.

Aunt Ann—Mother's sister—still going strong at ninety-eight!

We end up having a glorious day and early evening until Daddy decides he *has* to go to Main St. Café for a dessert of cake and ice cream. Keep in mind, it is Saturday night, and since it's the only decent restaurant within 25 miles, that place will be packed. I say this to Daddy, and he swears it's no problem. "Jimmy'll always find a table for me."

So, against my better judgment, off we go.

True to form, we get there and it is *packed*, with a long line of people waiting all the way out the door. I tactfully suggest we go home and eat ice cream and Oreos, but Daddy will have none of it: "Hell's bells…we're going in!" Like we're a fucking SWAT Team or something!

An important piece of this story is the fact that people suffering from dementia struggle with high anxiety and very short tempers, which is why *usually* when we set foot out of the house, I have a supply of Klonopin, an anti-anxiety drug, for situations exactly like this. However, for some stupid reason, I failed to put them in my purse before we left, and I am now stranded with a cranked-up dementia-addled grump and no Klonopin.

Shit, shit, damn, hell. I'm toast.

Daddy pushes his way inside—remember, he's ninety years old—and bellows, "What the hell are all you people doing here?"

Mortified, I try to pull him aside and quiet him, which of course pisses him off even more, and he hollers, "Where the hell's Jimmy? I come here almost every day—hell, I might as well own this goddamn place—and he sure as hell better find me a seat!"

Sure enough, in a few minutes, the sea parts, and here come Jimmy and a couple of his cooks out from the kitchen *with an additional table* and two chairs that they set down right in front of Daddy. "Here you go, Mr. Bill. Sorry you had to wait."

OMG. If looks could kill, all of us involved in that table scene would be dead. All these people who have been waiting for who knows how long now have to watch Grumpy Old Man get seated way ahead of them. Needless to say, they have murder in their hearts as they watch Jimmy fix up the table and seat us.

"That's better," grumbles asshole Daddy.

The waitress—another casualty in this story—comes over and asks what we would like to order.

"I want some of your chocolate cake with vanilla ice cream and a cup of black coffee," Daddy replies.

"I'm sorry, Mr. Boorhem, but we're out of chocolate cake."

Daddy starts shouting, "I can't hear you! It's too damn loud in here. What did you say?"

"I said, we are out of chocolate cake!" the waitress replies at the top of her lungs.

"Goddamnit, you are *never* out of chocolate cake. What the hell?"

"We've been so busy tonight we ran out!" she says, again, very loudly.

"Well, I'll be gawd-dammed. If that's not the shittiest service I've ever seen, I don't know what is."

By this time, *I* need a Klonopin. I would pay $500 for one if I could find a dealer, but there are none to be had. So, I put on my big-girl panties and intervene: "Shut up, Daddy! It's not her fault they're out of cake."

"The hell it isn't! Then whose is it?"

"Hell if I know, but *they are out of cake*, and you're not having cake. You can have ice cream and coffee, and we can eat Ding Dongs or Oreos when we get home. Jesus! Stop being such a dickhead."

He starts to argue, but I give him my best "If you say one more effing word, you are *dead*" look, and he thinks better of it.

"Bring me some goddamn ice cream then and black coffee." And then, looking at me with his famous go-to-hell look, he says, "And where did you get such a trash mouth? You shouldn't talk to your father that way!"

Unbelievable. I know he isn't self-reflective, but Jesus!

"No idea," I say. "And, by the way, you should not talk to your daughter—or anyone else, for that matter—how you just did!"

No response.

The shrinking waitress, witnessing all this, mumbles, "Yessir. Thank you, sir," and slinks off.

Poor girl. I bet she wishes she were dead right about now. By the way, the entire restaurant is watching, and people with murder in their hearts are still waiting to be seated.

But we eat our ice cream at the table that Jimmy brought out especially for us with everyone watching and secretly hoping that Daddy chokes to death on ice cream. He, meanwhile, takes his sweet time and drinks about ten cups of coffee. We *finally* leave. Ducking out the door, I leave the waitress a very large tip and give her the best "I'm so sorry" look I can muster. She smiles wanly back.

I told you he was mean as hell.

Once we get home and he's finally in bed, I think about opening a dusty bottle of wine I see in a very old wine stand and drinking the entire thing, but I sadly remember that I don't drink and really don't like wine. Instead, I snarf down three or four Ding Dongs—we have an unlimited supply—along with a very large glass of milk and crawl slowly upstairs to bed.

Thankfully, there are no middle-of-the-night shenanigans, and both of us get a good night's sleep. The next morning, seeking sympathy from my sibs, I'm on the phone with Beth and Ross giving them a blow-by-blow of The Night from Hell with Crusher Bill and no Klonopin—and me searching wildly through my purse for the magic bullet.

They, of course, are dying of laughter.

"You were not there!" I say. "It was not funny!"

"It's hilarious," they both say, "*especially* because we were not there!"

This family has no mercy.

The Birth of Crusher Bill

OF COURSE, MY FATHER WASN'T born with the name Crusher Bill. He was born June 18, 1922, in Los Angeles, California, to Lillian and Shelby Sr., christened with the given name William Boorhem—no middle name. He had an older brother by five years, Shelby Jr., with whom we were never sure how close he was.

His mother (Nonna to us) described him often by saying he could have been a clone of Mark Twain's famous character Tom Sawyer. With an impish grin and constant gleam in his eye (both of which remained till the day he died), he was full of mischief as a kid, constantly causing his caretaker, Stella, to cover his ass and hide his misdeeds and shenanigans. She called him Mr. Bill even when he was little, and there is no telling how many lies and misdirections she created to keep him out of trouble with Nonna. Stella probably reamed him out plenty for his sins, but of course

Daddy's mother, Lillian—Nonna to us, date unknown.

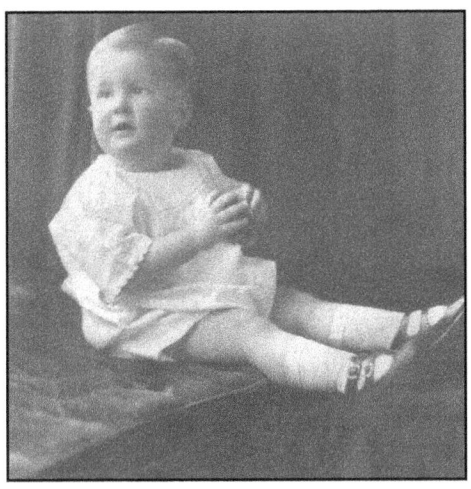

Baby picture of Daddy, circa 1923–24.

Daddy at age two or three, looking very serious.

she never really meant it: he was clearly the apple of her eye. She raised him and Shelby and then, when they were grown, raised all six of us!

Stella moved all over the country with Daddy's family during the 1930s. I asked him about moving so often (tied in with the question about attending so many schools), and he said that his mother had so much china and crystal that he and Stella had to pack up every time they moved—which was almost every year—that he would've just as soon smashed every "goddamn piece of that shit" as put newspaper around it one more time.

Until Daddy told me this story, I used to wonder why he never seemed to be attached to houses, boats, cars, or material things in general. He thought I was crazy to have such an attachment to my old house in Oak Cliff or my grandmother's house in Malvern, or especially that I named my cars. "That's the stupidest thing I've ever heard. Why in the hell would you do that?"

I thought he was just coldhearted until I pondered having to move so much as a kid and having to pack everything up every time; I realized I might be the same way. It also explained one of his famous Crusher Bill sayings: "Whatever you own, owns you!"

Nonna with Daddy in her lap and Shelby standing, circa 1925.

Daddy playing at being king—the role certainly suited him, circa 1928.

Daddy worshipped his father. Thanks to FDR, Shelby traveled up and down the Mississippi River overseeing and building bridges and roads to improve the infrastructure of the good ol' USA. Daddy went with him as a kid many times on these trips. He loved traveling with his father and especially loved all the huge machinery used in the bridge and road-building work.

There were the front-end loaders with huge jaws that literally moved the earth, massive steamrollers that could flatten a mountain, gigantic dump trucks that carried tons of rock and gravel, and Transformer-like conveyor belts that trundled rock uphill into the mouth of the actual rock crusher that ate it like candy and crushed it into limestone gravel for the base coat of roads.

Then there were the clumsy, lumbering concrete trucks, constantly stirring and shifting their load to keep it from settling, the

Daddy looking spiffy in his big-boy suit, circa 1927.

Daddy "ride-em-up-cowboy" looking like he owns the world, early 1930s.

skyscraper cranes used to move gigantic pillars and pylons, jack-hammers that took two to three men to operate, hundred-pound drills, grating machines the size of small houses to level the asphalt or concrete as it was laid over the gravel—he loved them all.

When I asked him how he got into the rock-crushing business, he described his times on the road with his dad as some of the best adventures of his life. He talked about the incredible power of the huge machinery, the blue-collar workers who looked and acted like such tough guys but were really just big teddy bears, and his fascination with how roads and bridges were built—he fell in love with all of it. The noise, the dust, the unbelievable power of machines cutting through the earth, the creation of massive structures and roadways. It's only natural that he would follow in his father's footsteps.

Daddy's father, Shelby Sr., circa 1930s.

Tragically, Shelby died when my father was only fourteen. I cannot imagine what that did to him because he never talked about it, but I do know that Shelby shaped my dad's life in profound ways—especially his choice of careers. I can still smell the dust from the rock crusher on Daddy when he came in from work every day, covered from head to toe in white limestone chalk. It was his second skin.

After WWII ended, Daddy went back to Malvern, married my mother, and went to work for his stepfather in the Malvern Sand and Gravel Company. The two never got along, and things went from bad to worse upon my dad's return.

According to sister Beth's intel from Mother, Frank was horrible, making my parents' lives hell. Among other things, he would call Daddy on Sunday mornings at 5 a.m., yelling at him to get his ass to the quarry with Frank's newspaper and coffee. I can imagine how well that went down with Daddy, and since he never was worth a shit working for anyone ever in his life, he was planning to buy land to start his own quarry. However, the scoop is that Frank, unbeknownst to my dad, bought up said land, ensuring his stepson could not go out on his own.

What a dick!

According to family lore, upon hearing the news, my grandmother—never a shrinking violet—beat the ever-loving snot out of Frank with a rolled-up newspaper for hurting her baby.

You go, girl!

With Daddy's options at a dead end in Malvern, not to mention the possibility of him finishing the job that Nonna started on Frank, it was time to get out of Dodge—that is, Malvern.

Nonna footed the bill for us to move, so Daddy up and took everyone (six kids, Mother, Stella, and probably a dog) away from my mother's hometown, her family, and all her friends, to Dallas, Texas, where they knew not one living soul, and went to work for a concrete company called Wesco.

Mother and Daddy's wedding picture—Daddy had only three weeks of leave, so the wedding was planned in overdrive! 1945.

Daddy looking dashing on the steps of our house in Malvern, Arkansas, circa late 1940s–early 1950s.

Daddy and his mother (Nonna) at Christmas on Gillon Ave—of course with the infamous ukulele, late 1950s.

Daddy, soon to become Crusher Bill, in Sherman, Texas, 1962.

Ross and Bill at Crushers, Inc., on a piece of rock-crushing equipment—I'm sure Mother did not know they were playing around the Rock Crusher!

It was there he met his partner in crime, best friend, and soon-to-be business partner, John Van Amburgh. To put it nicely, Wesco was not a good fit for either John or Daddy. They were both unceremoniously fired, booted out on the street with no money and fewer options. When I asked Daddy what in the hell they did after that, he said, "Well, we had two wives, ten kids, and no money between us, so we did what any sane person would do—started our own rock quarry."

That sounds *insane* to me! I mean, who does that with twelve mouths to feed, no money, and no credit? Well, evidently John and Daddy. I can just hear Mother's and Jody's reactions to that plan! I have no idea how they got the start-up money and probably don't want to know (I'm hoping it came from Nonna), but they went for it and grew that baby from one quarry on Lake Texoma to a multi-million-dollar business, naming it Crushers, Inc. Daddy was the operations guy, and John was the sales/dynamite guy.

Daddy at Crushers, Inc., office in Sherman. This is my all-time favorite picture of him, circa 1962.

So, Crushers, Inc., was launched, and Daddy was on his way to morphing into Crusher Bill. Daddy got the last laugh on Frank, too. In fact, thanks to Frank being such a dickhead, Bill Boorhem became one of the most successful limestone and aggregate producers in the state of Texas. His father, Shelby, would have been incredibly proud.

When you have a company called Crushers, Inc., and a personality like my father's—that of a steamroller and front-end loader combined—the name Crusher Bill would seem to be a natural evolution. But it didn't really enter our lexicon until we were in high school and my brother, Bill, went to work for him. Actually, Bill, Ann, and Beth all worked for him at one time or another, but it was Bill who was at the rock quarry sweating bullets, swallowing dust, and getting reamed out by Daddy on a daily basis. After several mishaps—I think Bill ran a rock-hauler into the conveyor belt at least once—causing additional upbraidings, he started calling Daddy "Crusher Bill."

Of course, that caught on like wildfire in the Sibling Network, and he was, from that point on, officially Crusher Bill. The funny thing is, I don't think he knew that's what we called him until many years later! How we pulled that off is beyond me, but one day I was giving him a hard time about who knows what and ended it with, "So, what do you have to say about that, Crusher Bill?"

He seemed genuinely surprised at being addressed as such, and I actually think I hurt his feelings a little bit. Who knows because he never said a thing about it after that incident, as usual, but the moniker stuck to him like glue until his dying day.

The Truckstop, the TP, and the Owl

I'M ON MY WAY TO the farm again, as it's my weekend for Daddy-with-dementia duty, and I start laughing to myself about a conversation Ross and I had last weekend when he was on the way to the farm for his Daddy-with-dementia duty. He had called to chat and pass the time on the road.

"What's up?" I asked as I answered the phone.

"Oh, not much. Daddy just called me and said he wants to go to Vivian tonight for dinner."

"Y'all gonna go?" I asked.

"Not too sure after what happened the last time Ann took him there."

Daddy all of a sudden *loves* this combo truck stop and gambling joint in a little town called Vivian, which is about an hour away from the farm. Why he loves it, I'll never know—he doesn't gamble, and although he says it looks like a real restaurant, I beg to differ. It's just plain ugly. Maybe it's because, like every other place over there, they all love him and fawn over him when he shows up.

One time when I took him, we sat down in a booth, and the waitress came over to greet us with, "Why, hi there, Mr. Bill!" Giving him a big smile *with no front teeth*—I am not lying—and big problems with the others, she asked, "What can I getcha?"

"Gimme some iced tea and a BLT with fries."

"You want sweet or unsweet tea, sugar?"

"Unsweet. Darlin' if I ordered sweet tea, they'd have to arrest me 'cause I'd be sweeter than the law would allow!"

"Oh, yewwww," she laughed. "Aren't you just the cutest thang?"

OMG.

"What the hell happened when Ann took him there?" I ask Ross.

"He stole toilet paper out of the men's room," he explains.

"What?" I ask, laughing hysterically. "He stole toilet paper? Why?"

"How the hell would I know? Ann said when Daddy went to the restroom, he came out carrying several rolls of toilet paper," Ross explains.

"Why on earth would he do *that*? Did he think we were out of it at the farm or something?"

"Again, *how the hell would I know?*"

I can't stop laughing picturing Daddy coming out of the bathroom with rolls of TP. What's even funnier, though, is imagining the look on Ann's face as she watched Daddy walk out of the bathroom—the pure mortification of watching her once larger-than-life father snarking toilet paper. OK, maybe it wasn't so funny, but I wasn't there, so I can laugh about it. Sure enough, when Ann saw him with the TP, shocked to no end, she incredulously asked, "Daddy, what in the hell are you doing with those rolls of toilet paper? You *have* to put those back!"

"Why the hell do I have to do that?" he asked, equally incredulously.

"Because they don't belong to you!" she explained.

"Well, shit. They were just sitting there being wasted. Might as well use them!"

So, Ross says, "Yeah, so no more Vivian Truck Stop for Pops."

"Well, you know this means the very next time I'm there, he's gonna pitch a fit to go," I complain.

"Yep, and good luck with that. I'm planning to get him drunk tonight, so he'll pass out and forget he asked."

"Oh, that'll work, especially since he *doesn't drink*," I say.

"I'll think of something."

So, my next time is now, and driving to the farm, I'm trying to come up with a plan to deter Daddy from wanting to go to Vivian. NPR is no help. "Surely he won't remember," I reassure myself.

As fate would have it, though, not thirty minutes after I get to the farm, Daddy says he wants to go to Vivian. I contemplate walking out the back door, getting in my car, and driving as fast as I can away from this backwoods part of the world forever. But then I remember that neither Earline nor J.J. are coming back until Monday. Unfortunately, I can't leave Daddy on his own that long—the house would not be standing by Monday.

"Are you *sure*? Weren't you just there the other night?" I ask.

"Yes and yes, but I like it and want to go back," he tells me.

"Well, I have no idea how to get there or how to get back, so *that's* a problem," I say.

"I know how to get there—I'll tell you how," he counters.

Oh, great. I can already picture us lost in bum-fuck-nowhere in pitch-dark rural Louisiana, driving around in circles with Daddy cussing a blue streak. Have you ever been on a back road in rural America? There is no light *anywhere*. The road sucks up your headlights and bounces your brights right back in your eyes, so they're no help. Varying sorts of creatures find it all of a sudden necessary to cross the road exactly when you come along, scaring the holy shit out of you, and depending on the size of the critter, if you hit them, you and your car are toast.

As my imagination goes wild running disastrous scenarios through my head, I'm dialing Ross's number to get some sense of where I have to go. He, however, is not much help as he doesn't remember road numbers or other small details necessary for my survival; he just "knows" how to get there. What fun. I'm totally on my own.

This is before I discover the sheer miracle that is Google Maps.

I finally say, "OK, but we have to leave by 4:00 so we can get back before dark."

"Fine with me," says Daddy.

We set off at 4:00, and miracle upon miracle, Daddy gets us there just fine. Problem is, it takes over an hour, and I'm now calculating that it will be nigh onto dark before we leave this hellhole, and once again, no Klonopin.

A different waitress from last time comes over, again all smiles, but she has all her front teeth and no problems with the rest of them. "Why, hi there, Mr. Bill!" she greets him.

"Hey, sweetheart. How are you?" he asks.

"Oh, I'm just peachy, and how are you, sweet thang?" Looking at me, she asks, "Weren't you just in here with Mr. Bill?"

"Uh, no...I don't think so," I reply.

"Well, I could've sworn I just seen you the other day!" she says.

"Oh, that must have been my sister Ann," I explain.

"Well, y'all sure do look alike!" she exclaims.

"True, but I am much younger and much better looking..." I say.

"Oh, yewwwww, you're just joshin'. Y'all could be twins!"

Before I can come back with a smart-ass reply, Daddy interrupts with, "How about some iced tea and a menu?"

Thank goodness she doesn't ask if he wants sweet or unsweet—I might have to throw up if I hear his "sweeter than the law allows" bit again.

Daddy orders meatloaf, mashed potatoes, green beans, and canned peaches. I get a BLT—the safest thing on the menu. We actually have a nice time chatting and eating our way into darkness—and to being lost forever on the back roads of Louisiana somewhere between Vivian and Belcher.

When we set out, it is indeed dark. I won't go into how dark it is in rural America again, but it is *fucking dark*. I ask Daddy, "You sure you can get us home? Should I call Lorenzo to come get us?"

"Hell, no, don't call Lorenzo. I know my way around here better than my own skin. We'll be fine," he maintains.

Ann and I looking twinsies at some Boorhem function, circa 1995.

Another example that Ann and I should have been the twins.

Shockingly, Daddy seems to be right. He knows every turn, which way to turn, and how many turns there are to get to the "main" road. As the tar drinks up my headlights, I begin to feel a bit more at ease and even start to believe we may actually make it home alive. Just about then, and again I have to say in the *pitch black*, I see (and almost feel) this enormously huge white barn owl, whose wingspan is, I kid you not, as wide as my Jeep is long, *swoop* down onto the road directly in front of us, pluck something off the road, and *swoop* back up into the ink-black night. I didn't even slow down, it happened so fast, and how that owl accomplished that maneuver without being front-end-loaded by my car will forever be an unsolved mystery to me.

"OMG! OMG! Oh. My. God. Daddy! Did you see that?"

"What?" he asks.

"That owl! That's the biggest bird I've ever seen! It just swooped down right in front of us and got something out of the middle of the road! Didn't you see it? A huge white owl?" I ask.

"Nope. I didn't see a thing," he replies nonchalantly.

"What? How could you not see it? Its wingspan was as wide as my Jeep is long!" I exclaim.

"Well, I didn't see it. Sure you're not hallucinating or something?" he asks.

"I am *not* hallucinating—that thing was real! I cannot believe I didn't hit it and you didn't see it!"

"Well, I didn't see a thing. And y'all think I'm the one with problems?"

Oh, good grief. Once again, I'm his "straight man." This happens all the time and gets really tiresome. I *did* see the huge-ass owl whose wingspan was as wide as my Jeep is long. It was enormous and it was *real. Daddy* is the one with problems, but thank the stars above, they don't include a bad sense of direction. We get home just fine.

As we pull under the carport, I say, "Damn, you're a pretty good navigator!"

Daddy replies, "And you're a pretty good driver. Let's just hope we're in the right goddamn place!"

Exhausted from the evening's adventure, by now I'm ready for bed! However, Daddy thinks, for some reason, it is imperative to call Ann and see how she's doing.

"Hello?" Ann answers.

"Ann? This is your darling father speaking."

"Yes, I know, Daddy! How are y'all doing over there?"

"We're just fine—got back from having dinner in Vivian a few minutes ago," he tells her.

"Cool. What'd you have for dinner?" she asks.

"Oh! It was great: roast beef, mashed potatoes and gravy, corn, green beans, and chocolate pie for dessert. Want to say hi to your sister?"

"Sure," she replies.

I take the phone. "Hey, Sis," I say.

"*Roast beef?* I didn't know they had that on the menu, or chocolate pie!"

Somewhat whispering, I reply, "They don't! Daddy had meatloaf and I had a BLT—no chocolate pie. I guess the damn meatloaf tasted like roast beef or something."

Ann starts howling with laughter and says, "Well, *good luck* with the rest of the weekend!"

"Thanks. You're no help."

I told you, *no mercy.*

Zac the Cat

NORMALLY I LOVE CATS. FOR most of my life, I have lived with cats and totally enjoyed their company. Daddy's cat, Zac, however, was a whole different story. He was my nemesis from the first day I showed up to serve Daddy-with-dementia duty until the very last. To put it succinctly, I hated that cat, and he hated me.

Daddy, on the other hand, *doted* on that cat. He had two dogs, but they stayed outside, and Zac the Cat was clearly the favored child among animals. According to Beth, he was originally Pat's cat, given to her as a kitten by Earline. He used to sit on her desk all day and keep her company while she worked. I guess when Pat died, he and Daddy bonded over their shared grief and became inseparable.

Zac was cute enough— black with two white paws and a white splash on his chest. He was small with short hair. Just a cat. But this was no ordinary feline. That damn cat was Houdini. He could disappear in the blink of an eye and be gone for hours, with Daddy all the while shuffling around the house calling in this hoarse

Zac the Cat—Daddy's love and my nemesis—also Ann's enemy, 2010.

falsetto, "Here, kitty kitty! Here, kitty kitty kitty!" nonstop. It drove both Ann and me nuts. Ann doesn't like animals that much anyway, and to have to put up with Zac's disappearing act and Daddy's constant search for him almost sent her over the edge.

One night, very late, Ann is upstairs and keeps hearing the garage door going up and down. This is a favorite trick of Daddy's when he is looking for the cat. He opens the garage door, shuffles down the driveway, and calls, "Here, kitty kitty!" nonstop until Ann comes out to stop him.

"Fuck! He's at it again." She goes downstairs, sees Daddy in the garage, and asks, "What are you doing, Daddy?"

"Looking for the cat," he replies.

"Daddy, the cat is not out here."

"How in the hell do you know that?" he asks.

"Because I made sure he was inside when we went to bed," she explains.

"Well, he mighta got out," he counters.

"Well, he might have *now* since you've opened the damn garage door."

"Then we've gotta find him."

"No, we don't. Come back inside—I'm sure he's in there," Ann says.

Miraculously, he comes back in and goes back to bed. However, Daddy does the garage-door-up-and-down trick two more times that night. Ann is pretty teed off by the third time she hears that stupid door going up and down, and she marches downstairs to give Daddy the what-for. She gets down the stairs, turns the corner into the office, sees Daddy, and shrieks, "Daddy! What. Are. You. Doing?"

Our darling father is standing *buck naked*, except for a pair of black socks, in front of Ann with his crowned jewels swinging in the wind. Who wants to see that?

"Oh my god! Daddy! Where are your clothes?" Ann shrieks again as she covers her eyes.

"I was hot," he says.

"Shit! You can't go around without any clothes on!" she shouts.

"Why not? It's my house," he replies.

"Because I don't want to see that! What are you doing down here again anyway?" she asks.

"Looking for the cat."

I'm proud of Ann for not decking him on the spot, but she probably would have missed anyway, with her eyes covered as they were to block the scene in front of her.

"Zac is *not* outside. Go put your pajamas on and *go to bed*!" she instructs.

"How do you know that?" he asks.

"Because he's *right here*," Ann proclaims as Zac comes sauntering into the office.

"Well, hell."

I'm telling you, trying to find that cat was like looking for a needle in a haystack. He could fit in the weirdest places, get out of the tiniest openings, find something to hide in right in front of your eyes, and generally wreak havoc with his absence. One day when it's my weekend at the farm, the yard guys show up to mow the lawn. Daddy starts pacing around, getting really anxious, and starts calling for Zac. "Here, kitty kitty!" Dad calls about ten times before I ask, "Daddy, what's wrong?

He replies, "I can't find Zac, and the yard guys are here. What if he's outside?"

"I'm sure he's fine, even if he is out there."

"No, he's not! They might chop him up with their goddamn mowers or run over him if he's hiding somewhere!" he exclaims.

"Daddy, they are *not* going to chop him up. Have you looked inside for him?" I ask.

"Hell, yes, I've looked inside. He's not here. And how do you know they won't chop him up? They're not looking out for him."

"OK, but let's see if he's inside. Did you look in your room?"

"No, I did not look in my room. He is not allowed in my room! I *always* keep that door shut, so he can't go in there," he tells me.

"Well, maybe we should look anyway, just to be sure," I suggest.

"I'm telling you, he's not in there, goddamnit! He's outside, and those idiots are gonna kill him!"

"OK, but before we totally panic and storm the yard guys, I'm going to look in your room. Is that OK with you?"

"I guess, but you're wasting your damn time," he says.

I go to his room and open the door, and out walks Zac.

Daddy: "Well, I'll be goddamned."

I go eat four Ding Dongs and silently curse that no-account cat.

Besides searching nonstop for Zac, Daddy liked to look for imaginary animals he thought were either in the house or out in the yard. There were many times that we were looking for *two* cats, not just Zac.

"I know I have two cats," he tells me.

"Daddy, are you sure? I only know of one—Zac."

"No, I have another one. Can't remember its name, though."

"Are you sure you're not thinking about your two dogs?" I ask.

"Hell, no, I'm not thinking about my dogs. I know the difference between cats and dogs. I'm not a dumbass!" he snaps back.

"I know that, Daddy. I was just wondering."

"Well, OK. But I need to go outside and find that other cat."

Jesus H. Here we go again. Whenever we go out into the yard, I have to hold Daddy by the back of his pants—which he hates and for which he cusses me out every time—because he won't use the beautiful cane I bought him or his walker, and he could easily take a tumble.

"OK, but you know I have to hold on to you," I remind Daddy.

"Jesus Christ—I'm not an invalid," he says.

"I know you're not, but I'm holding on to you anyway."

"Oh, shit. All right. Let's just go!"

Out the back door we go, down the garage steps (very slowly), down the driveway, and out into the yard. While we're puttering around looking for the nonexistent second cat, Daddy decides he needs to fill up the dogs' water bowl. "I'm gonna put some water in their bowl." (Really a very large bucket.)

"OK, but let me help you," I say.

"I don't need any goddamn help—you just hold on to me, and I'll do it."

So glad no one was there videoing us, with him bent over wrestling the water faucet to turn it on, and me breaking my back giving him a wedgie so he doesn't land head-first into the water bucket. Plus, it's hotter than hell.

"Daddy, hurry up. My back is killing me!" I complain.

"I can't hurry up. Just let go of me," he instructs.

"I'm not letting go of you to watch you take a dive into the water bucket."

"I'm not going anywhere—I've almost got it," he says.

He finally gets the faucet turned on and fills up the bucket. It takes another act of God to get the faucet turned off, and then we pick up our puttering where we left off searching for the nonexistent cat. After looking under various and sundry possible hiding places, Daddy surmises, "Well, I'm probably not going to find that other cat."

"Why not?" I ask.

"Because I don't have a second cat."

I clamp my mouth shut in the broiling heat to avoid screaming at the top of my lungs, "I *told you*, you don't have a second godforsaken cat!"

Instead, I just say, "Huh. Well, I guess we better go back inside then," and we putter back through the garage up the steps and into the house.

Five minutes later while eating another three Ding Dongs, I hear from the office, "Here, kitty kitty! Here, kitty kitty

kitty!" I stuff a fourth Ding Dong into my mouth to drown out the noise.

ZAC THE CAT WAS A country cat. He loved chasing squirrels, climbing trees, digging in Earline's flowers, tormenting Jetta and Lacy (the dogs), and, of course, tormenting me.

The only time Daddy "used" the cool cane with a racehorse head on it that I bought for him. He eschewed help with walking almost to the end.

Zac would crouch inside the screen porch eying some poor bird or squirrel he had in his sights, and then suddenly, he'd be *gone*—and so would that bird or squirrel. I never figured out how he got out of the screen porch—nary a hole could I find large enough for him to get through. But Houdini that he was, he escaped nonetheless and wreaked havoc all over the yard.

He should have lived in the barn with the horses, he was such a good hunter. No mouse could have survived his watch, but Daddy would have none of that—Zac was a house cat and his baby and could do anything he damn well pleased—except, supposedly, go into the bedroom. You know how well that went.

Every time I was there, I tried diligently to never let Zac out of the house. Invariably, though, someone left a door open just long enough for him to snake through and evade my grasp. I dreamt way too many times of chasing that cat all over the house and yard, only to come up empty-handed time after time—dreams reflecting the reality of my life at the farm. He definitely had the goods on me.

Now that I think of it, he probably *was* down at the barn on his many hours-long forays, mocking us all as he played King Cat for a day, rounding up all the mice. Lorenzo never said anything about seeing him down there, but why would he? Zac was the invisible marauder that none of us could ever find unless he wanted to be found.

But oh, how he loved Daddy. Lap-sitting was his favorite pastime, and he and Daddy would spend hours in the recliner napping, watching TV, and just hanging out. Seeing how much they loved each other almost made me like him a couple of times—until he'd pull another disappearing act, and I'd have to follow Daddy around again, mewling after that damn cat.

Zac turned my father from a dog person into a cat person. Quite a feat, considering Daddy *always* had dogs around him. He brought them home from the pound, from the Rock Crusher, from a friend, from anywhere. Most of them didn't stick, but

Lady, our collie/shepherd mix was his favorite, and she grew up with all of us. She slept with Ross in the "dungeon"—basement bedroom—but it was Daddy who got her trained, bred her (please note, however, that it was Mother who dealt with the birthing and raising of the puppies), and constantly fed her the forbidden scraps under the kitchen table—well, Beth did, too, but Daddy did most of it.

We would bring home kittens and cats, but Daddy was never as fond of them. He did, however, fish a bunch of kittens, birthed by Bridget the cat, out of the oil pan of the coal-oil furnace we had for heating. That was fun. Of course, it was Mother who bathed them and made sure they didn't die of oil poisoning—if that's a thing. That was how it was. Daddy brought home the strays, and Mother ended up saving them.

I take after my dad in this regard. I've rescued so many dogs, it's ridiculous. Like Daddy, most of them didn't stick, but my Australian Shepherd mix, Millie—who leapt into my car when I yanked her out of the middle of a busy street, intending only to move her to the grass—was with me a very long time.

I've rescued my share of cats, too, but usually because they wandered up to my porch and stayed there. We had one who lived under our very old house and who would stick her head up in the floor vents and *howl* for someone to come save her. Another one got stuck under the porch, and we had to saw through the porch floor to get her out. Our rescue, Cleo, loved to stretch out on top of the air-conditioning unit while the fan was blowing. I had visions of her getting sucked down into that thing and cat fur and guts flying everywhere.

Leslie also had a cat named Zac, who was a flat-faced Persian. Why I thought getting that kind of cat was a good idea, no one knows. Poor thing. I'd get a big fat F in taking care of him. Every six months, we'd have to get him shaved, he'd be so matted up from lack of grooming. Also, a mighty hunter, he did *not* want to stay inside—thus the lack of grooming. One time, I had to

Harriet and Ross with two of the many animals brought home by Daddy, circa late 1950s.

pull a string out of his butt—*do not try this at home*—which I should not have done, but miracle upon miracle, it came out sans intestines or other organs.

Over one of the many school holidays, Leslie got to keep the class bird at our house. That was a *big* mistake. One afternoon, I came through the front door to see Leslie's Zac under the dining room table with bird feathers coming out of either side of his mouth. I swear, it was exactly like a cartoon—I was totally appalled and grossed out but could not help but howl with laughter. Thank God Leslie was not home to see and hear me do that—she would have been traumatized for life. That cat jumped up on the refrigerator, opened the bird cage, and murdered and ate poor Tweety Bird. Try telling your classmates *that*. I pulled

Barbra with Punkin the cat, yet another rescue, late 1950s.

Ann with Murphy, one of Daddy's
surprises.

The original Lady, Lake Bridgeport, 1950s.

myself together to deliver the tragic news appropriately when Leslie got home, and she, of course, was devastated. But like a chip off the old block, when I told her about the feathers in his mouth, she had to giggle. We never did find a carcass and were forced to fess up to the teacher and buy another class bird, one that *never* stayed at our house!

Tragically, Leslie's Zac was killed by a dog that should never have been in my yard—a crime for which I never forgave my then partner or myself for letting happen, and for which I'm sure Leslie never forgave either of us. I keep a picture of Leslie's Zac on my fridge as a reminder of the consequences of laissez-faire animal parenting and having a totally irresponsible person in your life.

Leslie's Zac.

Daddy and Ross right before Ross's wedding ceremony, when he was still trying to be straight. The marriage didn't last, but Ross and Pat are still dear friends.

Ross (C) and Pat (R), with Pat's sister Karen (L).

Pat and Zac, 2014.

We buried Leslie's Zac in the ever-growing pet cemetery in our backyard, which, by the way, is totally illegal in Dallas, Texas. Having lived in that house a very long time, we amassed quite a burial ground for pets gone over to the other side. Throughout the years, whenever I would mention wanting to sell the house, Leslie, even into her young adult years, would wail, "No, Mommy, no! We can't leave the animals!"

But I digress. Daddy's Zac the Cat was a Heinz 57. Daddy used to say that was the best kind of dog, but I guess it applies to cats, too. Zac seemed impervious to any illness, danger, or

Daddy and his beloved Zac, 2012.

mishap that could have befallen him at the farm. He was healthy as a horse and probably would have lived to a ripe old age had he not gone to live in the city after The Year of Grace. Sadly (and I do mean that), he maintained his escape-artist skills, got out of the house one too many times, and met his demise at the hands of a reckless driver in a very-much-larger-than-Zac car.

I hate to think about that, even if he was my nemesis. No poor creature deserves that kind of death. He was living with Ross's former wife, Pat. Yes, I know I told you he is gay. They married before he came out, and it obviously didn't last, but they've stayed great friends throughout the years. She is a bona fide animal worshipper and so was kind enough to take Zac in. I'm sure she was brokenhearted at his loss and gave him a fitting burial. I take solace in that.

Zac about to jump up into Daddy's lap for one of their napping sessions, 2013.

As my sister Barbra said, "Zac was not cut out for the city. He was used to his freedom at the farm." Unfortunately, the perils of city life did him in, and he was transported to kitty heaven. He and Crusher Bill are probably having a fine time laughing at all of us down here and our many attempts to tame them both. Like my dad, Zac was quite a character. Also like my dad, he caused a bunch of people around him a bunch of trouble and never thought twice about it. God love 'em both.

Bad Harriet

DADDY AND I ARE SITTING on the screen porch one evening "visitin'" while I show him pictures on my phone of his kids, grandkids, and great-grandkids. Interestingly, he recognizes all his kids and some of his grandkids. When I show him a picture of Leslie, my youngest, he asks, "Who is she?"

"Daddy! That's Leslie, my youngest. Remember, you named Leslie's Love after her, and remember how devastated she was when the horse got claimed?"

"Oh yeah, now I remember. Well, she doesn't say much for the character of your genes!" he says.

"What in the hell do you mean by that?" I ask.

"She doesn't look like you," he replies.

"Oh. Well, she looked just like me when she was little but now has a lot of her dad in her."

"Which one was he?" he asks as he chuckles to himself.

My father never missed a chance to harangue me about the too-many men in my life, and this jab was no different. In fact, the men in my life were the top reasons he and I had so much conflict and tension between us. From my high-school summer flame—"that weirdo"—all the way through to my last long-term guy—"worthless as a piece of shit"—my dad was never short on criticisms regarding the men I chose to be with.

A man was, in fact, the reason for my first banishment from the family. My father disowned me twice in total. Both times I was never sure if he actually cut me out of the will, but he definitely played his *you don't exist and are invisible to me*

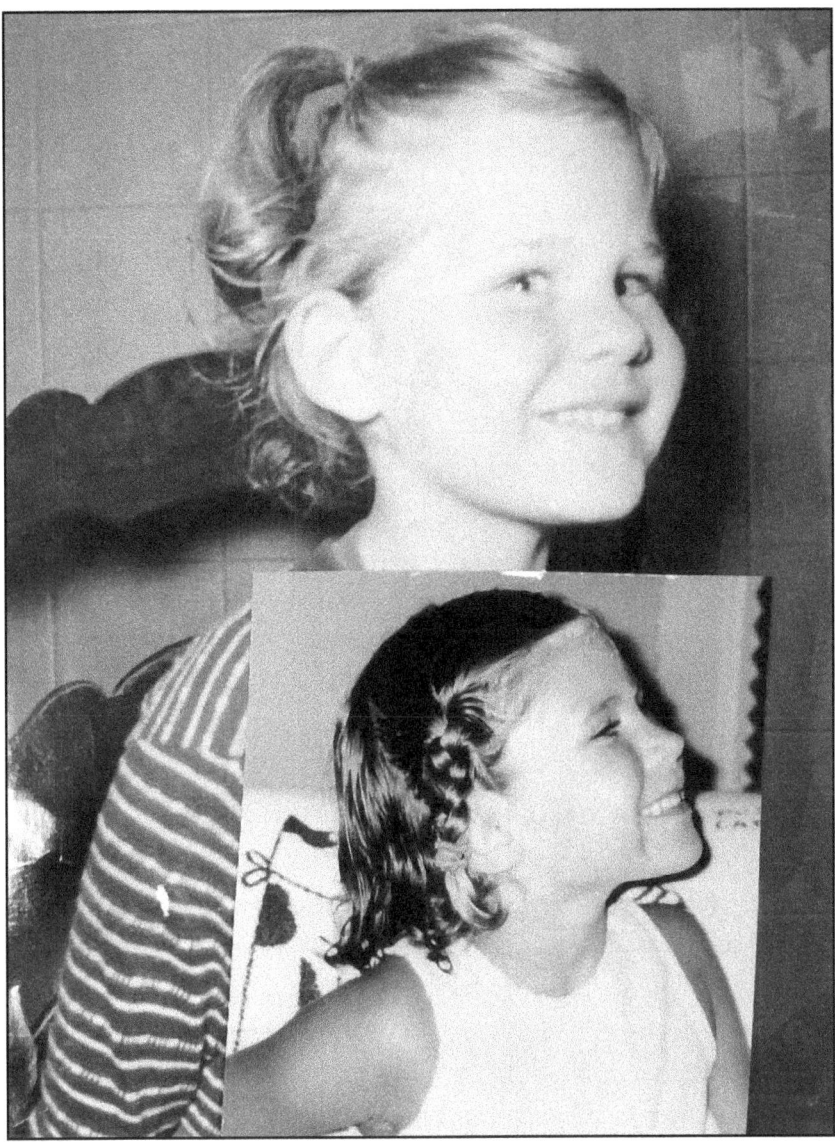

Comparison of Leslie and me at four years old; I'm in the top pic, and Les is in the bottom. She looked just like me till she was about eleven or twelve, 1955 and 1995.

game, which played out as no cute phone calls from Daddy, no invitations to visit, me being completely ignored by him at family functions, him talking shit about me to all my siblings, and complete and utter disapproval of my existence. Each episode lasted from several months to several years and ended with no explanation or closure. He would simply decide to honor me with his presence—via phone call or "dropping by" my house.

He was a hard man.

The first time was just stupid. I was dating my future husband Stuart, and we decided to move in together. This was in the 1970s, right after the "free-love" sixties, which my father abhorred with all his might, partially because that was when my brother Bill got into so much trouble. Hardly anyone in those days got married before living together, but to Crusher Bill, it was worse than a mortal sin. He was apoplectic when I told him.

"Why in the hell would you do a thing like that?" he roared.

"Because it's a good way to see if we're compatible enough to get married. Everyone does it, and besides, my first marriage ended badly, so I'm being cautious," I explained.

"I don't care if the *Pope himself* is doing it. You're a complete and total dumbass if you do this!"

"Why on earth would you say that?" I asked.

"Because you're handing him his cake and letting him eat it, too—forget about him marrying you—why would he do that when he can have everything he wants without the commitment?" he asked.

"Stuart doesn't think like that! That's terrible of you to say!"

"The hell he doesn't! Any man thinks like that, and you're an even bigger dumbass than I thought if you think differently," he callously replied.

"Times have changed, Daddy. It makes no sense to marry someone without living with them first," I said.

"Times have not changed one bit, darling. Marriage changes everything even if you have lived together for a hundred years! Living together *does not* equal being married."

"How the hell would you know? You've never lived with a woman before marrying," I challenged.

Right before my wedding to Stuart, 1978.

"I know because I'm a man and I know how men think. We will do and say anything if we think there's free sex involved. Don't be so damned naïve."

At least he didn't call me a whore, or trash, or a kept woman. He was quite clear, however, that I was a dumbass and an idiot and that I was totally naïve when it came to men. And, of course, he had to add that my mother would be horrified at the prospect.

I should have known he'd react that way. He hated all my boyfriends except for my high school sweetheart, George, and really hated my first husband, which in hindsight, I can't blame him for, and I probably should've been disowned for marrying him!

I kicked myself later for not using my tried-and-true modus operandi of saying nothing and just quietly going about my business. He probably never would have even known that we were living together.

But I had entered my "therapy years" and was spending hours with my therapist slogging through the shit with my family. Self-help was the zeitgeist of the '70s, and I bit hook, line, and sinker, trying to heal the pain of my family relationships—particularly those between my parents and me.

I did it all: Transactional Analysis, Gestalt, Psychoanalysis (this was before my feminist awakening and rejection of everything Freudian), Drama Therapy, Carl Rogers's Humanistic Therapy, Group Therapy, Group Intensives, Weekend Therapy Retreats—anything and everything that had a chance of making me feel better.

The only thing all that therapy really did, though, was to make me mad at my family and act like a total ass to them, which did not help my interactions with my father regarding Stuart. I was bent on standing up to him and "owning my power," which got me absolutely nothing but the cold shoulder and his ire until Stuart and I married.

He warmed up after our wedding, and actually, Stuart became his favorite of all the men I was ever with. He *loved* retelling the

Young me on my honeymoon with Stuart, 1978.

story of the night he and Pat got married, and Stuart ran over his own leg with his coveted Corvette while trying to put it into park for the valet guy. He thought it even more hilarious that I wouldn't go to the ER with Stuart, telling him, "I'm not missing this wedding. You're on your own!" Daddy was furious with me when I told him we were divorcing. I'm not sure he ever forgave me or that he ever stopped missing Stuart. He would ask about him every time I saw him and *always* reiterate how much he liked him: "Only decent one in the bunch."

Thanks, Dad.

Mother's high school graduation picture; I see all four girls in this picture of her, 1938–39.

My beautiful mother, Jane, circa late 1940s–early 1950s.

During my mother's battle with cancer, he once again became intensely unhappy with my behavior. I was pretty much MIA during a lot of it, which thoroughly pissed him and my siblings off. My rationale: I was a newlywed, trying to build a life for myself separate from my family, working full time, spending a *lot* of time in therapy, just trying to find myself. At least, that's what I told myself.

The truth was, I wanted so badly to be close to my mother, but that had never happened. I totally blamed her for that, and so I was unbelievably angry and hurt. I thought if I admitted to myself that she was terminally ill and let myself witness her decline, all hope of any connection with her would be lost. So I chose to stay in la-la land and pretend life was normal. But of course it wasn't, and because of my being MIA, I was once again on Crusher Bill's shit list. I remember him bellowing at me as he was reaming me out about my lack of presence at the farm, "Your mother *got up out of her sick bed* to attend your

Mother and Daddy at an unknown function. This is one of my favorite pictures of Mother—she was filled with grace and beauty.

wedding in 110-degree weather, and *this* is how you repay her?" I have no idea what my retort was, but I'm sure it was fairly smart-assed.

I did start making appearances at the farm on the weekends to help Mother do her nails, wash her hair, take baths, shave her legs—all the feminine stuff the women in my family love to do. We never talked about anything important: she never once mentioned her illness (which made me apoplectic at the time), never talked about the possibility of her dying...nothing. We spent time sitting on her bed doing all the girly things and pretending we were OK. And that's as close as I ever got to having a relationship with my mother.

She died when I was four months pregnant with Kat, my oldest. I remember my father calling me right before I was heading out to my regular OB/GYN appointment and him saying, "You go to your doctor's appointment and take your time getting here. There's no rush."

That's all I recall from that day—I don't even remember driving to Sherman—except walking through the farmhouse door and seeing Sadie, the dog I had given them, lying in the hall by Mother's room. She knew something weird was up.

That whole time is a blur, including the graveside service, about which I remember very little. What I do remember is us girls going through Mother's things, seeing who would want what. I was the only one her size—feet, too—so I ended up with many of her clothes and shoes.

I realized years later what a desperate attempt that was to hold onto our very tenuous relationship and keep some of her with me. I had so much unfinished business with her about which I would never get closure that I was grasping at whatever would keep me connected to her.

It actually helped, as did many years of good therapy. But it wasn't until years later when I sang "Lux Aeterna" from the Rutter *Requiem* in concert with the Women's Chorus of Dallas and The Turtle Creek Chorale that I was able to lay her to rest. "Light Eternal," sung in the magical space that is the Meyerson Symphony Hall, lifted the past from both her and me and allowed her to finally fly with the angels and me to let her go.

I now remember my mother fondly, am grateful for all she did for me and my sibs, understand her sadness and depression, admire her incredible ability to scare the shit out of six teenagers, wish like hell she could have been the artist she was meant to be, and stand in awe of her strength, grace, and beauty. When I think of her, I hear her tinkly laugh, see her beautiful smile, and hear her saying, "Oh, look, Harriet! The dogwoods are blooming!"

AFTER MOTHER DIED, I MADE two life-changing decisions. I divorced Kat's dad and went back to school to become a therapist.

Mother and Daddy in Atlanta during my "Bad Harriet" days. They were gorgeous. Circa early or mid-1970s.

Her dad and I were, like everyone else, in therapy at the time, and when I told my counselor and him that I wanted to go back to school—I was working for Southwestern Bell at the time and making lots of money, which Stuart loved—she asked him what he thought about it. He said, "Well, I guess I'll just have to divorce her." He was not amenable to change. He did eventually come around to the idea, but by then it was too late. I beat him to the divorce punch and moved to Commerce, Texas, with my then three-year-old daughter to finish my bachelor's, master's, and doctoral degrees. It's too bad he was so hung up on money—we really liked each other—but it was what it was, and it was over.

Crusher Bill agreed with Stuart and thought I was crazy to quit a great-paying job, and that I was especially crazy to divorce Stuart, move to Commerce, Texas, and buy a house, no less. I quote: "The only reason I'd buy a house in that godforsaken town was if I was gonna *die* there."

I did it, though, so the money I got from the divorce wouldn't go straight down the apartment rental drain, which turned out to be a *great* decision. I not only kept my money, but I also rented out my house after moving back to Dallas and used it as a tax write-off for several years. Not such a dumbass, after all, huh, Daddy?

Still thinking I was crazy, however, he *could not* get his head around the fact that I wanted to be a therapist: "Why the hell would you want to listen to other people's problems? You've got enough of your own to deal with!"

Then, one day when I was at his house in Dallas, I started telling him a story about one of my clients who really was crazy. He went berserk. "You are a complete dumbass to deal with those kinds of people. What makes you want to do that? What is wrong with you?"

That pissed me off, so I retorted, "What the hell is wrong with *you*? 'Those' people need help just the same as anyone else. What is your problem?"

"One of those crazies is gonna kill you one day."

Oh! Then I got it. Crusher Bill code for, "I'm worried about you." Surprise, surprise! My father worried about me. I needed to write that down in the record books.

"No, Daddy, no one is going to kill me. There's no danger, and I'm never alone in the office, so if I need help, someone is always there. Besides, we have a security guard to help out if needed," I explained.

"Well, hell. You just better be damn careful—you never know."

"I will."

And that was the end of that. He never understood my career choice but did, after many years, come to respect me as a professional. Good enough.

For the rest of my adult life, until shortly before I started Daddy-with-dementia duty, my father and I continued to have a distant, tense, and strained relationship. It eased somewhat when I had Leslie because Pat fell in love with her and would have her stay at the farm for a week at a time. I used to meet them halfway between Belcher and Dallas at this BBQ joint outside of Longview to do the handoff. Leslie loved going over there, of course, because Pat spoiled her rotten and bought her anything she wanted, and she got to play with Earline's daughter, Shannon, the entire week.

On the way to the farm after one of our handoffs, Leslie (still in diapers) had a giant pooptrastrophe—her diaper mightily runnethed over—all over Pat and, according to Daddy, all over the car. I never heard the end of that story—you'd have thought she had shit all over his face or something. Pat didn't mind one bit, though, angel that she was. She made him stop at the next gas station and cleaned everything up. Daddy, of course, did not lift a finger to help—typical. His role, as always, was to micromanage Pat's changing of the diaper and tell her all the ways she was doing it wrong. Typical of Pat, she told him in no uncertain terms to back off and went about the business of making Leslie presentable again.

Also typical of my father was that when I came alone to do the switch with Leslie, Daddy was friendly enough; however, if my then-partner came with me, no dice. He was, as always, highly critical of my choice and never hid his displeasure. That was a barrel of fun, let me tell you.

But when I became CEO of a large nonprofit in Dallas, my credibility with Crusher Bill took a big jump. He was the kind of father who never told you to your face that he was proud of you, but he told everyone he knew that I was now large and in charge and how proud of me he was. That used to fry my ass that he wouldn't tell me, but eventually I let it go and decided I had better things to be mad about.

I gained so much credibility with Daddy by being in charge that he donated lots of cash to my nonprofit, played in its golf tournament, participated in a Boorhem Family Gift Giving party for the agency, and actually said out loud what a great organization it was. He even met some of the kids we served, ate dinner with them, and took a tour of the agency, which may not sound like such a big deal to you, but my father was a capitalist to his core. He thought anything that was not done for profit was worthless, and he espoused the old "pull yourself up by your bootstraps" mentality. So, for him to endorse, contribute to, and even participate with a nonprofit entity was a major signal to me that I was off his shit list.

Then, when I became single for the final time, my father warmed up considerably. Now, as a therapist I could find all kinds of uncomfortable meanings in this, but I choose not to go there. Suffice it to say, I was back in his good graces. Of course, it helped that I was much more relaxed around Daddy as a single person than when I was connected to a man, so who knows what the real story is? All I know is that things got better and pretty much stayed that way, which is why agreeing to get into the rotation to take care of him was not that difficult.

War Stories

Daddy in his Navy flight gear. He and I look so much alike, it's kinda scary! 1943.

MY FATHER WASN'T PRONE TO self-disclosure. He was much more comfortable cussing out the most recent SOB, pontificating on the ills of the world, telling jokes and stories, or telling you how you should live your life. He used a million "sayings," which we dubbed Crusher Bill Sayings, when telling a story or cussing you out. And of course, his favorite, "Dumbass!" all of us heard at one time or another.

Daddy flying one of the larger WWII bombers.

WWII Corsairs were flown from land bases by the Marines when they were deemed too unsafe to fly from naval aircraft carriers. They began flying off carriers in 1943 after the kinks were worked out.

The Corsair fighter plane flown by the Navy off of aircraft carriers once they were deemed safe enough. Daddy flew them from 1943–44.

Aircraft Carrier USS *Rudyerd Bay* that Daddy flew Corsairs off of.

Naval Air Training Center
Pensacola, Florida

Know all men by these presents that

Ensign William Boorhem, A-D(N), U. S. Naval Reserve

has completed the prescribed course of training and having met successfully the requirements of the course has been designated a

Naval Aviator

In Witness Whereof, *this certificate has been signed on this   2nd   day of   May, 1944   and the Seal of the Naval Air Training Center hereunto affixed*

Commander, U. S. Navy
Superintendent of Aviation Training

Captain, U. S. Navy
Commandant
Naval Air Training Center

Daddy's Naval Aviator Certificate.

Daddy's Naval Aviator Certificate to fly the Corsair, circa 1942–43.

Daddy in his Navy whites, circa 1943–44.

Daddy in his Navy whites, 1943.

Daddy post-WWII and his years in the Naval Reserves—so handsome.

Daddy—always a patriot, circa 1925. Daddy in his Navy flying gear, 1943.

Harriet in Daddy's Navy
hat, summer 2022.

As famous as Crusher Bill's sayings were, he didn't have any about the time he spent fighting in WWII. He did, however, have plenty of stories. We talk about "war stories" to describe difficult experiences or situations we've found ourselves in, but most people who actually fight in a war and live to tell about it, don't. I've never met a person who fought in a war and was excited to share the experiences, and Daddy was no different. He would never just offer up stories about the war, but strangely, if you asked, he'd answer any question.

I wish I had asked a lot more because growing up I knew very little about his wartime experience. I knew that he was a Navy pilot and was in the South Pacific. I also knew that he would not buy a Japanese-made car for decades after the war ended and that he hated anything that was not made in the United States. I knew that he had little desire to travel to foreign parts and that his favorite saying about that was, "If you're leaving this country, you'd better be goddamned sure you have a roundtrip ticket." He unabashedly loved "America the Beautiful" and had little tolerance for other countries. He was most definitely an elitist when it came to which country was the best on the planet, and he was *not* a world citizen—he was an American citizen through and through.

So, of course, when the United States entered WWII, my father enlisted. Because he had been to college for a year, he was admitted to the Naval Officer Candidate School to train as a Navy fighter pilot. He was twenty years old and soon to be a Top Gun.

Young, brash, cocky, and brave, he loved every minute of flying. He flew a variety of bombers and fighter planes, large and small, but his favorite was the F4U Corsair. One of the best fighter planes of WWII, the Corsair tormented the Japanese from Guadalcanal until the end of the war.

His favorite plane was powered by a Pratt and Whitney R-2800 Double Wasp 18-cylinder engine producing over 2000 horsepower. It's hard for me to believe that he ripped through the skies at more than 400 mph in that bird, the United States' first single-engine

WWII Corsairs, the plane Daddy flew and loved, 1944.

fighter plane to do so. It was not just fast but also incredibly deadly, armed with six .50 caliber M2 Browning machine guns, which he would have operated himself all while dodging the enemy.

Designed initially as a carrier aircraft, problems with the landings forced the Corsair to land-based duty until the issues could be fixed. It was so dangerous, in fact, that it was nick-named "Ensign Eliminator" because of its tendency to flip once it hit the carrier. Lt. Commander Sam Porter tested the feasibility of operating the Navy's bent-wing fighter from the deck of the escort carrier USS *Sangamon*. After four terrifying landings, he called it quits, certain the airplane was on the verge of killing him. Because it was so incredibly difficult to land, it did kill many young, less experienced fliers than he before it was pulled from carrier duty. Luckily, Daddy was not one of them.

He began flying Corsairs in 1944—when they were finally allowed to operate from US Navy carriers. Even with improvements, the fighter was never a pussycat during landing. Green pilots still found ways to slide, bounce, or flip their Corsairs in those vulnerable seconds of final approach. But when the bugs were ironed out, the Corsair hit its stride. The venerable "U-Bird" went on to become one of the best naval fighters of WWII, racking up 2,140 victories in aerial combat. It was at Okinawa that the Corsairs were given the nickname "Angels of Okinawa" due to their success against Japanese aircraft.

To think that my father was part of these history-changing battles is mind-boggling. One time my sister Beth asked him if he was ever scared before taking off on a mission. He replied, "Nah. I'd sit in the briefing room, looking around at all the guys and wondering who wouldn't be coming back. I damn sure knew it would not be me—I was coming back, no matter what." And he always did.

My father entered the military as an ensign and was promot-ed to lieutenant junior grade during his tour. He served on the Aircraft Carrier *Rudyerd Bay*, the 27th of fifty Casablanca-class escort carriers built for the United States Navy. She served first as a replenishment and transport carrier and later as a frontline carrier, providing air cover and support for the invasion of Iwo Jima and the Battle of Okinawa. Daddy flew torpedo bombers and fighters off her deck, having received flight training for both.

During the last year of the war alone, my father racked up over 800 flying hours and an untold number of missions. He flew solo—terrifying to imagine—in Corsairs, operating the machine guns and bombs single-handedly, and piloted full crews in the larger fighters and bombers. I stay amazed that any of them got out of that hell alive and stand in awe of their courage and dedication to their country. They truly do not make many like him anymore.

I tell you this to let you know what a badass my father was. He flew the most dangerous fighter plane of WWII and relished it. Along with that, he flew torpedo bombers and fighter planes of various sizes. He flew long-range special radar search missions and air-cover missions for both the invasion of Iwo Jima and the Battle of Okinawa. He was truly a Top Gun. Although all the WWII fighter pilots were extraordinary, only the best of the best flew Corsairs because of their difficult handling and nasty landing behavior; Crusher Bill was most assuredly one of the best.

I never knew the Corsair was a fighter plane till I was grown. My father never boasted about his talents as a fighter pilot or about how many planes he shot down; I just knew he loved flying and loved being in the Navy.

He did tell us, however, that he was shot down twice.

"Wait, what?" we asked.

"Yeah, had to put her in the drink a time or two."

"What! Where? WTF?" More than stunned, we listened raptly as he told us the tale of his being shot down in the Pacific and living to tell about it.

Not one for details, all he said was, "We got hit, we were going down, did a bellyflop in the drink, and were picked up by a submarine."

Again we asked, "What? How did *that* happen?"

"Well, we landed her and waited on the wing to be picked up. I felt something underneath us like movement and thought at first that it was a shark. Turns out it was the submarine breaking surface."

"Wait. It came up *under* you? And what do you mean, 'we'? There were more than just you in the plane?"

"Oh yeah. We had a co-pilot, radar guy, gunners, a bombardier," he explained.

"Did you lose any of them?"

"We lost a few," he said. Jesus Christ. He was telling us all this like he was talking about the weather.

"What happened next?" we asked.

"Well, the sub picked us up.

"How did they know where you were?"

"Hell if I know. I guess radar. I can sure as hell tell you this, though. Putting that baby in the drink was *nothin'* compared to being on that goddamn submarine for a week. That will make you nuts," he said.

Turns out he was claustrophobic. It had to be bad if it was worse than crash-landing a plane in the ocean!

Full crew and a plane full of bombs and ammunition, he landed it without the entire thing blowing to bits in the take-no-prisoners Pacific and lived. And even better, after he got off the submarine, he went back to flying as if nothing had happened.

I didn't hear about the second time he was shot down till much later at the farm. He was far into his dementia journey by then, so I wondered if it was even true until I heard from several of my sibs that he had told them about it long ago. There were even fewer details about this crash-landing except that he swam to shore.

"Wait. You *swam* to shore? What shore?" I asked.

"The Philippines."

"The Philippines! Daddy, that was Japanese territory! How did you keep from being captured?" I asked.

"Oh, it wasn't a problem. We had pretty much taken the island by then." And that is all he said. Again, like he was talking about the weather.

———

Mother working in Washington, DC, during WWII, 1943.

Daddy (far left), Mother (far right), Aunt Ann (next to Mother), and unknown others, probably in Washington, DC, sometime during the war years.

AFTER MIRACULOUSLY SURVIVING BEING SHOT down twice and upon completing four years of service to his country, my father was honorably discharged from the Navy. Upon landing in the good ol' US of A, he and his buddies went on a two-week bender in San Diego before going home to Malvern. He did not tell anyone he was back in the States, wanting to be free to party till he dropped—which he did.

After the extended party, he flew home sporting a two-week hangover and landed in Little Rock. His mother picked him up from the airport, and according to him, the following exchange occurred when she saw him: "Oh my god! You look *horrible*! What have they done to you?"

"I don't know what you're talking about. This is just what being in a war does to you, Mother."

Upon hearing that, she burst into tears, sobbing and holding him, crying, "Oh, my poor baby!"

So typical. I'm sure he milked that for all that it was worth!

———

FROM THE WAR'S END THROUGH 1956, because my father loved the Navy, he served as a pilot and flight instructor in the US Naval Reserves. He was promoted to lieutenant and got to keep doing what he loved best—flying fighter planes. Since they were no longer at war, he and his cronies found it necessary to cook up some mischief to keep Reserve life interesting.

One assignment required my dad and seven other pilots to fly eight fighter planes from the East Coast to Naval Air Station Dallas in Grand Prairie, Texas. The flight pattern took them over Arkansas, his home state, and right over Malvern, where my mother and all of us kids were. As they crossed over the Arkansas line, Daddy was flying right point and signaled to the other pilots that he was taking the lead and to get ready to "Say hello to Jane and the kids."

Certificate of Daddy's appointment to the Naval Reserves, 1949.

At right about Little Rock, they all dive-bombed down in formation low enough to buzz Pine Bluff Street in Malvern, with Mother and Barbra standing out in the front yard! Daddy said they were low enough to wave, which I'm sure totally freaked my mother and sister out. Can you imagine seeing *eight* fighter planes dive-bombing little Malvern, Arkansas, flying right down the middle of town with pilots waving as they roared way too low overhead and then shot back up into the sky?

"Are you kidding me? You didn't really do that, did you?" I asked.

"Hell yes, we did that."

Incredulous, I continued, "But *how*? How did you not hit something—run into power lines, get electrocuted, hit someone, chop off trees?"

"We knew how to fly, that's how."

"Jesus H.! Did Mother know you were going to do that?" I asked.

"Of course not. I just decided to have a little fun," he said.

"Did you know she was going to be in the front yard?" I asked.

"How in the hell would I know that? No. That was just an extra bonus."

"And the other guys just said, 'Sure, let's go for it'?"

"Oh sure. They were always up for a little diversion," he chuckled.

"What happened after that?"

"Nothing. We went on to the naval base in Grand Prairie."

"Did you get in trouble?"

"Nah, not really. But we did get a lot of press—most of it not so great."

This was better than TV.

Another weekend assignment had Daddy and four other pilots transporting fighter planes from the East Coast to Naval Base San Diego. This trip, the flight plan took them over San Francisco. Guess what's in San Francisco?

Yep. According to my father, things had been a little dull in the Reserves lately, so they planned to have a little fun on this trip. Once again, they decided that flying high in the sky wasn't that great, so they flew. Under. The. Golden. Gate. Bridge. Then they looped up and around, did it again, and then did it a *third* time.

Wonder how many car wrecks, boat crashes, heart attacks, and life-long traumas that caused the good citizens who just happened to be crossing over or under that bridge on that certain day? Daddy swore there were no such injuries, but who the hell knows?

"You are two kinds of liars," I accused him.

"Hell if I am! We flew under that bridge three times."

"Then you're just truly insane."

"We might have been nuts, but it was fun," he said.

"So did you get in trouble *this* time?" I asked.

"Well, that depends on if you call almost getting court-martialed trouble."

Maverick. Idiot. Show-off. Maniac. I could go on and on.

But that was how he lived his entire life. Rules meant little to him. When I was graduating with my bachelor's degree, we had to drive to Commerce, Texas, from Dallas for the ceremony. The traffic sucked, there was only one route, and we were going to be late. So, Daddy took it upon himself to "blow this joint" and swerved onto the right shoulder of the road—going about sixty mph, by the way—and got around all the traffic, honking at anyone who wouldn't get out of his way. That was especially fun on bridges! Of course, we got there on time, and miraculously, no one died, although all of us except him were complete wrecks.

He piled up so many speeding tickets traveling between Sherman and Bridgeport, Texas, where his two Rock Crushers were, that they had a warrant out for his arrest. One time he asked Beth to wash his car, and when she opened the glove box, it was *stuffed* with tickets. Horrified, she asked him about it. His reply? "The speed limit's too damn low."

When he and his best friend, John Van Amburgh, were driving to Fayetteville one weekend to see the Arkansas football game, he turned to John and said, "Goddammit, I sure wish I had that baby grand piano of Jane's that's sitting in the living room right about now."

John, taken totally by surprise, said, "What the hell are you talking about?"

Daddy shot back, "If I had that piano, I'd have the goddamn football tickets that are sitting on top of it!"

Did they get into the football stadium? Of course they did. How did they get into the football stadium? No idea. Where there is a Crusher Bill, there are no rules and there is always a way.

With his distaste for rules, how he survived the Navy—and why he stayed in—is still a mystery to me, although to be fair, he did almost get court-martialed. When I looked through his Navy file, it seemed to me that they wanted Daddy to be a lifer, and that could be why they promoted him in the Reserves. He might have obliged them had he not had a wife and six kids that it would be pretty tough to move around the world every year or so.

Maybe he didn't want us to go through having to move a billion times like he did as a kid, or maybe he didn't want to have to move all over the place again. Who knows? But we were the reason he gave on his discharge papers for leaving the Navy.

I can't imagine moving every year or so. Moving from Dallas to Sherman was traumatizing enough for me. I was eleven years old when Daddy turned our lives upside down and yanked me from my cozy, happy, idyllic world to the hostile territory of Sherman, Texas. He had opened Crushers, Inc., on Lake Texoma and didn't want to commute from Dallas. On the way to Sherman, driving up Highway 75, I vividly remember turning around in the back seat, gazing at the Dallas skyline and vowing to get back there as soon as I could, which did not help my adjustment to Sherman one bit.

I'm not sure I ever forgave him for that move until one day at the farm when I was telling him about a trip back to Malvern I had made recently.

"Didn't you start school there?" he asked.

"Nope. Only Bill did. The rest of us started in Dallas," I said.

"Boy, that was a step up, huh?"

"Yep, but then a major step down when we moved to Sherman! I hated that place," I told him.

"What? I thought it was OK."

"Uh, no. I was traumatized for life because of moving there," I said.

"Oh, come on. Really?" he asked.

"Yes! I was so traumatized, I started stuttering again."

"Well, I did feel sorry for you having to change schools," he said.

"What? You never told me that!"

"No? Well, I did. I went to so many schools, I knew how hard it was. Come to think of it, I guess it *is* something to start stuttering about!"

Wow. Just. Wow. Remember those corrective emotional experiences I told you about? This was one of them. To hear him say that he actually worried about my well-being transformed my perception of him. My father actually thought about me and—even better—*worried* about me. I forgave him instantly, which then caused me to re-evaluate my time in Sherman in a more realistic light and remove it from my shit list. It wasn't that bad after all. I really did have some great friends and great adventures there, but that's for another time.

Top Gun Bill finally said *bon voyage* to the Navy at the end of 1956. I was five years old, and we had already moved from Malvern to Dallas. None of us kids had any idea that he stayed in the Navy for as long as he did until we were grown. That is so baffling to me: that we lived with this man every day growing up and never knew a large chunk of his history—a chunk that he told me several times later were some of the best years of his life.

Stella and Earline

Two women deserve their own chapter in the Year of Grace—Stella and Earline. Key players in Daddy's life at vastly different times, they played essentially the same role—that of caretaker, friend, maid, housekeeper, enabler, and devotee. They both worshipped my father, would do anything for him, and put up with his ridiculous shenanigans, his filthy language, his racism, and his inappropriate humor. Both were with him at vulnerable periods of his life, and both mothered him like their own. Stella raised him from a young age, and Earline cared for him in his old age. Like bookends to his life, they held the beginning and end of his existence between them.

The irony is not lost on me that my father, racist that he was, was more deeply connected to two Black women than to most of his children. I don't really know what to say about that except I'm glad he had those profound connections. I know that he genuinely loved both women and probably would have been lost without them, and I also know that his relationship with them was in no way equal. Although they gave him the "what for" many times, he was always the boss and always the privileged white man. Both called him Mr. Bill, Stella doing so even when he was a little boy.

As his children, we followed right along behind our father in totally loving both women. Each came into our lives at different times, and each played important roles in our well-being. Stella mothered us when we were little, and Earline mothered us when we were adults. Both were outstanding cooks, and we still talk

Stella with Shelby, 1917.

Stella with all of us. Ross is by her, then L-R: Ann, Harriet, Bill, Barbra, Beth. No idea where we were, but we always looked like a bunch of street urchins!

about Stella's rice pudding and Earline's many baked delicacies. Earline still brings us all kinds of goodies when she comes to visit.

In many ways, my father owes his life to these two women. They sacrificed a lot to be sure he was taken care of both as a boy and as an old man. He was incredibly lucky to have two women who were strong enough to throw his abuse right back at him yet nurturing and loving enough to be the ones he wanted with him in his last moments.

I don't have many stories about either woman, but I want to acknowledge them and their undying loyalty to him. Stella and Earline, the alpha and omega of his life.

Stella

Stella was born during a time in history when it was not uncommon for Black women to spend most of their lives working for white families and raising their children. She did just that and

Daddy's brother, Shelby, with wife Maria Helena and their sons, Edward, Shelby, and Robert, mid-1950s.

is an icon in our family lore. Stella mothered not only Daddy and his brother, Shelby, but also all of us until we were almost teenagers. At the end of my father's life, it was her he called for. She ranks with the angels in the Boorhem family history book.

Daddy adored Stella, bailed her out of many a scrape, and took care of her until she died. I went with him to her funeral in Dallas and witnessed first-hand his true devotion to her. He was genuinely grief-stricken as he gave his condolences to her family, shared stories of her life with them, and sat in the family pew during the service. It was truly moving for me to watch.

As we sang about, prayed over, and memorialized Stella that day, I thought back to my earliest memories of her. The most vivid one occurred when I was about three years old. I was in the backyard of our house on Mockingbird Lane, digging in the dirt with an old spoon, when I suddenly had the great idea to go visit a friend who lived down the alley. "I know the way," I surmised to myself. "I'll just go down the alley to visit for a bit!"

I headed out the back gate to start my trek, and shortly thereafter I got lost. I don't remember being scared or frightened. I do remember wandering around until I walked up into some family's front yard as they were having a picnic lunch under a tree. A nice woman saw me and offered me a Coke. I have no idea what she might have said to me or asked me, but in no time, up drove a Highland Park Police car that pulled into her driveway. Out stepped an officer who picked me up and deposited me into the front seat of his car. The only thing I remember about that ride was how huge his gun looked to me and how far away from me on that long bench seat he was.

I guess Mother or the woman with the picnic called the police because he knew right where to take me. As we pulled up to my house, there were Mother, Stella, Ross, and Lord knows who else standing in the front yard waiting for me. I got out of the car and made a beeline for Stella, not my mother. I jumped up into her arms and heard her say, "Lord, Chile, you scared us all half to death! Where you been?"

Shelby and Daddy, 1922.

Shelby, Daddy's brother, circa early
1950s.

Daddy (L) and Shelby (R), circa 1924.

Shelby (L) and Daddy (R), circa 1926.

Nonna's mother, with whom she did not get along and who skipped Nonna in passing down furs and jewels to Shelby Jr.

Nonna with Beth, Harriet, Ross, Ann, and Barbra some Easter. We had no idea of the real story of why Shelby moved to Brazil then.

L-R: Shelby, Stella, Daddy—Shelby's farewell visit, late 1950s.

"I wanted to see my friend," I told her.

"Don't you never do nothin' like that again! You'll turn yo' momma's hair white!"

She hugged and hugged me, and I held on for dear life. I remember nothing from that point on. I guess we went inside, and life resumed as usual, but I still think it's telling that I went to Stella first, not my mother. Evidently, Stella wasn't the only thing I held on to for dear life. I still had my spoon in my hand!

The other early memory I have of her relates to the farewell visit my Uncle Shelby made to Dallas to see Daddy and my grandmother, Nonna, when he had been diagnosed with lung cancer. Like his father before him, Shelby would die before he reached the age of fifty, and this trip from Brazil to Dallas was his swan song.

Daddy always told us that Shelby moved to Brazil to work for Texaco, but when Ross and I visited Shelby's wife, Maria Helena, several years ago, we got the real scoop. Evidently, Nonna and her mother did *not* get along, and when her mother died, various expensive furs and jewels, along with quite a bit of cash, went straight to Shelby Jr. instead of Nonna because he was the eldest grandson. Of course, Nonna did not like that and asked Shelby to give the stuff to her, feeling she was the rightful owner. When he would not, she *took him to court* to get it back. Can you imagine? Suing your own son? He won the suit, but not before losing everything his grandmother gave him to pay the stupid court costs!

Wow. I'd move to Brazil, too. He did get an offer from Texaco to work in Brazil and met Maria Helena there, but had Nonna not been such a witch, he might not have jumped so quickly at the chance. According to Daddy, Shelby broke Nonna's heart when he left, and she never recovered. Served her right, as far as I'm concerned. She told us a *very* different story about why he left, making us think he was the villain, breaking her heart and splitting up the family. All those years of us thinking Shelby was the bad guy, when all along, it was Nonna who was so awful.

When we asked Maria Helena if she ever told Daddy any of this, her reply was, "Why would I? Why would I want to destroy the image he had of his mother? He loved her very much. At that point in his life, there was no need to disrupt that." She was a better person than I would have been, and how did my father not know what happened? Shelby was only five years his senior—surely they weren't *that* disconnected—but Maria Helena swore Daddy never knew the real story of why Shelby went to

Daddy's mother, Lillian Boorhem McGillicuddy—Nonna to her grandkids, date unknown.

Brazil. She also told us that Nonna pestered her for years about the furs and jewelry and never believed they were sold to pay court costs. Wow, again. Parents can really suck.

I guess Shelby came to Dallas to mend fences with his mother and see his brother one last time. I remember Stella being instrumental in his care on that trip because he could hardly eat anything, and she fixed all his meals especially so he could. Rice pudding, cornbread crumbled in milk, mashed up vegetables and meat, different soups and custards, and I don't know what else. I can imagine how difficult that was for her, seeing him so ill after missing him those many years.

I remember thinking he was very handsome, polite, and quiet, but that's about all. I remember nothing about everyone's interactions, what activities they may have participated in, or how long Shelby was there. I'm sure the visit was quite tense and difficult for all of them and extremely taxing on Shelby. How horrible to know this would be the last time you'd ever see your brother or your son or your mother again? So tragic. We have a picture of Daddy, Shelby, Nonna, and Stella in the front yard of our house during that visit, and none of them look very happy. I can certainly understand why.

Whether or not Nonna went to Shelby's funeral, we never knew. I know Daddy did not. He never talked about that visit again, or Shelby, unless we asked specific questions. Besides losing his father at such a young age, I consider this to be one of the saddest stories of Daddy's life—one that still holds a myriad of unanswered questions that will haunt me forever.

AS DADDY TOLD IT, STELLA always carried a knife. Evidently, she ran in some tough circles when she wasn't taking care of us and, per Daddy, "would just as soon cut you as look at you." Geez Louise! Our sweet Stella a gangster? What a scary and exciting thought!

He claimed to have bailed her out of jail more than once for fighting and her husband, Arthur, for drunk and disorderly behavior. Of course, we didn't know this until we were much older and Stella was no longer working for us, which is probably a good thing, as we would have hammered her with questions and gotten all of us kids and Daddy in big trouble. I always wondered if Mother knew about any of this. It's hard for me to believe she would turn a blind eye to such behavior, but Stella continued to take care of us years after we moved to Dallas.

Stella worked for my grandmother and my father during extremely racist times. Segregation was deeply entrenched throughout the country, especially in the South, and stayed that way as long as she worked for my family. Although Daddy loved Stella dearly, he was just as racist as the next guy and held a pretty low opinion of Black people as a whole. He bought into all the stereotypical adjectives used about them at the time, and if I were a betting person, I'd bet he was not in favor of integration. He also never bought into the notion of Black people as an oppressed group, holding fast to the belief that anyone could make it in this world if they wanted to.

I have often wondered how Stella managed when Daddy and his parents moved all over the place. On the road, where did she sleep? Where did she eat? Did she have to stay in the car at restaurants? What about hotels? I really wish I had asked my dad much more about Stella's life with them and what it was like for her during those times. Of course, he never talked about it—whatever happened, I'm sure he thought it was completely normal at the time, and Stella probably did, too. That doesn't make it right, though.

The relationship Stella had with my father and our family is what I call *benevolent racism*. What that meant was although you were racist regarding Black people as a group, as long as they knew their place, worked hard for you, took care of your kids and your family, stayed polite, and were available any time day or night, you took care of them. They became part of the family, albeit never equal members, and they were looked after for the rest of their lives by your family. You could talk all the shit you wanted to about Black people around them, because "Of course we don't mean you," and expect them to spend more time with your family than theirs, be available for holidays and vacations, and basically indenture themselves to you. Most importantly, they didn't exist outside of your family.

Here's how this played out with Stella: every one of my brothers and sisters and I loved her to death; however, we never knew her last name, never knew she was married until we were older, never knew if she had kids, never worried about her being at our house all weekend or on holidays, and never knew if she went to church or what she liked to do when she wasn't with us. She was there fixing our breakfast every morning and there at dinner every night. She took us fishing with the other Black maids in the neighborhood and watched out for us during the day. She waited with my mother at the corner when we came home from school. Outside of our family, she was invisible to us. Her only persona was Stella, our maid, our surrogate mother with no last name. As well as we knew and loved her, we knew *nothing* about her as a real person.

She was just always there. She spent every weekend, every holiday, probably every vacation with us. I'm sure she lived in a house separate from us, but we had no idea where it might be. For all intents and purposes, she lived with us. We never thought about her as separate from our family or as having a life outside of us. She never talked about it, and we never asked. It wasn't until I was much older that I learned more about her life, and only then because I pumped Daddy for information. Significantly, and sadly, I still don't know her last name.

Earline

I do, at least, know Earline's last name—but I didn't until I asked my brother just the other day, and probably the only reason he knows it is because he manages the family trust from which she gets a stipend. You see what I mean? Benevolent racism—it was still alive and well in 2022. As embarrassing as that is to admit, it's important to fess up to my own racism and privilege, even as I work to dismantle it.

Earline worked for Daddy and Pat during supposedly more progressive times, but Belcher, Louisiana, missed the memo to update their diversity and inclusion manual. Consequently, time pretty much stood still when it came to how white folks thought about Black folks, including my father's attitude. When he was still able, Daddy walked at the mall in Shreveport for exercise and lamented to me one time about the plight of "mixed babies."

"First of all, where are you seeing all these babies?" I asked.

"At the mall—I see them in strollers when I'm walking."

"And what do you mean, 'mixed'?" I asked.

"You know..." he hesitated.

"No, I don't. What do you mean?"

"You know, part white and part Black," he said.

"Ohh! You mean they are of mixed race? How on earth can you tell?" I asked.

"Because they are either lighter or darker than their mothers," he explained.

"Good grief, Daddy. That doesn't mean anything. Lots of babies have lighter or darker skin color than their parents. And so what if they are mixed? Why would you feel sorry for them because of that?"

"Because they don't stand a chance in hell. They'll be ostracized their entire lives," he said.

"No, they won't! Times have changed, Daddy!" I told him.

"No, they haven't, at least not in Belcher, Louisiana."

Daddy, Earline, and Pat at Foxwood.

Daddy with his great-grandson—
Andrea and David's son—Luke,
adopted from Thailand, circa
2002.

Earline's girls, Kyra and Shantazia, with Popio's great-grandchildren Luke, Sebastian, and Bailey.

"You'd be surprised. Leslie has several friends of mixed race, and it's no big deal."

"Maybe not in Dallas, but it matters here," he said.

"Daddy, stop making assumptions," I told him.

"I'll assume all I want, and I'm right. Those babies have a hard row to hoe. And on top of being mixed, most of them probably don't even know who their fathers are."

"Now you're *really* making assumptions. You do not know that," I said.

"I'd bet money on it."

I hope he never had that conversation with Earline, but it would not surprise me one bit if he had. As usual, his beliefs had a grain of truth, but that's about all. Pulling from his own life experience, he never felt obligated to update his beliefs as times changed, even when mixed-race children became part of his family. Life was very black and white to Crusher Bill, and

Easter egg hunt at the farm.

mixing colors just wasn't an option for him. He hated for the food on his plate to get mixed together, and he felt the same way about race. Sadly, the beliefs that were imprinted on him as a kid never changed.

Despite having to deal with my father and all his crap, Earline was such a breath of fresh air! Every time I'd show up at the farm, she'd holler, "Hi, Miss Harriet!" even though I told her to drop the "Miss" a million times! "I'm *so* happy to see you! You look *so* beautiful!" she'd go on, no matter how terrible I looked.

There were always at least two made-from-scratch chocolate cakes she'd baked and sometimes homemade cinnamon rolls or breakfast pastries. I don't know how I didn't gain fifty pounds that year because I constantly had some kind of very fattening food in my mouth. If it wasn't Ding Dongs, it was Earline's delicacies or Chips Ahoy! cookies. Obviously, Daddy was a chocoholic, and Earline gladly enabled him, big-time!

Along with worshipping my dad, Earline *loved* Leslie. She spoiled her rotten just like Pat did, let her get away with murder, fed her anything she wanted, and generally doted on her. When Leslie visited the farm, Earline's daughter, Shannon, would come stay, too. Shannon was about five years older than Leslie, so of course, Leslie thought she hung the moon.

Earline used to tell Shannon before she would come to stay with Leslie, "Now, don't go fixin' your hair in some weird do, 'cause you know Leslie's gonna want me to fix her hair just like yours." Leslie had really curly hair, but it was not hair you could make into an Afro, and making it look just like Shannon's was nigh on impossible, but Leslie would *insist*. One time Shannon came over with her hair up in a fabulous poof that Leslie begged Earline to imitate with her hair. As hard as she tried, Earline, of course, could not make Leslie's hair poof like Shannon's. After about thirty minutes of trying, she called it quits, and Leslie had to face the hard truth that she had white girls' hair that was never going to poof like Shannon's. But if Shannon sported braids or a top knot or anything besides a poof, Earline *had* to do Leslie's hair the same way.

Besides being Leslie's idol, Shannon was instrumental in teaching Leslie to drive—way before she was old enough. How they managed it, I'll never know, but Shannon—also too young to drive—put Leslie on her lap in the truck and drove all over the farm with Leslie steering and Shannon working the pedals.

According to Leslie, they drove past Lorenzo many times, waving and honking the horn, with no repercussions. When Leslie got older, Shannon said, "Oh hell, just drive—your feet reach the pedals." So she did! Again, all over the farm, with no alarm bells sounding.

I have so many questions about this that will never be answered because Leslie won't divulge how girls too young to drive had carte blanche to bounce all over Foxwood in a beat-up pickup truck. Earline denies any knowledge, and no one else is around to interrogate. I wouldn't be surprised if Daddy gave them the keys to the truck himself to get them out from underfoot—kind of like the bad joke of sending your kids out in the traffic to play—since he had little tolerance for "kid noise." Besides, he learned to drive at an early age, so he probably thought nothing of it.

I can just hear him: "What the hell could happen on a farm?"

"Oh, nothing. Just things like driving into the lake, running into cows, turning over in a ditch—little things like that," I imagine I'd reply.

"Oh hell. That's not gonna happen. They'll be fine."

"So *you* say," I would reply.

Evidently, he was right because nothing bad ever did happen, and Leslie is an excellent driver. Maybe it was that farm driving!

Earline and Shannon were such important contributors to Leslie's love of Foxwood and of spending time there. They were so generous with their time and affection, making sure she had a great time. Leslie and I owe them both a deep debt of gratitude. Tragically for Earline and for Leslie, Shannon died at the young age of twenty-three from an aneurysm. Pregnant at the time, she fell into a coma and never revived. Earline made the horrifically difficult decision to keep her on life support until the baby could be delivered full-term and then to discontinue life-extending measures. A healthy girl was delivered, and Shannon died several days later. The baby was named Calissa and was adopted by Earline's niece. Unimaginable. Earline, Pat, Leslie, and the entire family were devastated.

Shannon's death left behind three daughters. Earline adopted the two oldest girls and raised them as her own. Now beautiful young women, Shantazia and Kyra are a testament to Earline's incredible ability to parent through her grief and raise smart, poised, and confident girls. Shannon would be so proud of her daughters and of her mother.

Pat and Earline were especially close. Pat worked in the office off the kitchen, so she and Earline would gossip and talk shit about everyone, including Daddy. Of course, he would talk shit right back, as in this conversation about Earline's blue jeans:

"Earline, what in the hell is wrong with those pants?" he asked.

"What do you mean, 'what's wrong?' Nothing! Why?" she countered.

"Well, hell, they're all ripped up! Did you fall down or something?"

"Of course not! Ripped jeans are in style. Keep up!" she said.

"That's the stupidest thing I've ever heard. Who in the hell would want to wear jeans with *holes* in them? You could at least put some patches on them."

"Don't be stupid. That would ruin the entire look. Right, Miss Pat?"

Pat always agreed with Earline, to my father's chagrin. It took them both to keep him in his place and out of Pat's farm-running business and Earline's personal business. He was, by his very nature, incredibly nosy and always wanted to know the latest gossip. At dinner, he'd cross-examine all of us about the latest goings on with our friends and neighbors, what was happening at school, who was dating whom, who was friends with whom, who was on drugs or drinking too much, who was pregnant—his thirst for the scoop was insatiable and never waned, even in his old age. He loved a good story. The juicier, the better.

Earline was always full of news—about everybody and everything. I think that's why Daddy loved her so much. He could always depend on her to liven up his day with a good story. Her family was a goldmine. Being one of *twenty-two* kids—by the same parents!—meant there was always some kind of drama unfolding with her brothers and sisters with which she could keep him entertained for days.

As with almost every woman he ever met, my father was incredibly crass with Earline. One morning, I overheard him on the phone asking her what time she was picking him up for a racetrack party: "When are you coming to get me?"

"Well, I have to get dressed first," she told him.

"Well, come nekked, and then it'd be a *real* party!"

"Mr. Bill!"

I couldn't understand the rest of what Earline said, but it was very loud and had a most chastising tone to it. He deserved it. No court in the land would have denied her a considerable settlement for sexual harassment upon hearing that exchange. I chewed him out for talking to her that way, but Crusher Bill was impervious to criticism—in one ear and out the other, as they say.

There wasn't a woman within my father's range of sight upon whom he did not comment. At dinner one night with Ann, a woman with rather large breasts at a nearby table got up to go to the restroom. Daddy ogled her and said way too loudly to Ann, "Would you look at the titties on that woman!"

"Daddy! Shut up! Where are your manners?" she admonished.

"To hell with manners. Just look at them!"

If Ann could have gotten up and left him there, she would've. He had no shame when it came to his always-unasked-for opinions. Another night they were at Main Street Café, and Daddy just had to comment on a plus-sized woman at the salad bar: "I want you to look at how much salad she's putting on her plate!"

"Daddy, it's only salad. What's wrong with that?" Ann asked.

"At her size, she should be eating air pudding and wind sauce!"

"OMG. You are unbelievable!"

At Kountry Kitchen one morning, I was the lucky one who got to hear his commentary. We were seated in a section of the restaurant with several tables of military personnel. He, of course, was checking out the scene when a female officer stood up to leave. "Jesus! That Army girl should be playing defensive end for New Orleans! She's big enough to take down the entire front line by herself!" he exclaimed.

"Daddy, hush! You're being way too loud and very sexist! Want her to come over here and defensive-end you?" I asked.

"I'm not being sexist. I'm just telling it like it is! Besides, she can't hear me," he said.

"I don't care that she can't hear you. I can hear you and am totally offended!"

"Oh, quit being so serious. You need to lighten up."

How many women have heard *that* line before? He was hopeless—totally in one ear and out the other.

Another night at Main Street, a young couple entered and were waiting to be seated. The young woman was plump, to say the least, and sported a crop top and very short cut-off jean shorts. Her derriere was much exposed, as was her midriff. I thought Daddy was going to fall out of his chair. Luckily, all inappropriate remarks by Crusher Bill were spoken out of her earshot. He did, however, spend the entire evening stealing glances at her and then conspiratorially whispering those inappropriate remarks in my ear.

We finally left and had an uneventful drive home. When we got there, I said I was going to put on some shorts and hope I looked better than the young woman we saw earlier. Daddy quipped, "Darlin,' there is no way in hell you could ever look like that hussy."

OMG.

About two hours later, I heard, "Ross! Ross! Where the hell are you?"

I skyrocketed out of bed and found Daddy at the foot of the stairs hollering for my brother.

"What is it, Daddy?" I asked.

"Where's Ross? I need him to do something for me," he replied.

"Daddy, he's not here. I'm here with you this weekend."

"Well, shit. When's he coming back?" he asked.

"Next weekend. Can you wait till then for his help, and can we go back to bed now?"

"Well, hell. I guess so. By the way, you're sure short on clothes there!" he said.

"Daddy, I was in bed! These are my pajamas!"

"They're a little skimpy for pajamas, aren't they?"

"I always wear shorts and a tank top to bed," I told him.

"Well, at least you look better than that Main Street hussy!"

Dear God, he's never going to let that go, I thought.

MY FATHER WAS A LADIES' man, to put it nicely. In addition to commenting on every woman he saw, Crusher Bill probably propositioned most of them. He was horrible. I wouldn't be surprised if he had propositioned Earline at one time or another. Had that happened, she would have knocked him flat and told Pat, so if he was smart, he kept that option off the table.

He was not above trying to pinch her butt, however. Upon one occasion in the kitchen, when he pinched her, Earline cried out very loudly, "Miss Pat! Will you tell Mr. Bill to stop pinchin' my butt?"

To which Daddy replied, "Goddamnit, Earline, why'd you have to do that?"

"Because you're being a dirty old man!"

"I am not. I'm just playing," he said.

"Well, you can just stop playing with my ass—it don't belong to you!"

Even after Pat died and at the ripe old age of 86, he was looking for women. To stay virile, we found out later, he was scarfing down daily Viagra. Ann found out first during one of her and Earline's many discussions about Daddy.

"Yep. Your dad almost passed out right in front of me," Earline told Ann.

"What? How did that happen?" Ann asked.

"No idea. He stood up from the breakfast table, turned white as a sheet, and almost passed out."

"What did you do?" Ann asked.

"I made him sit with his head between his legs and called the doctor."

"Did the doctor say why he got so dizzy?"

"Mr. Bill has been taking Viagra every day! Supposedly, it can make your blood pressure really low, and that's what happened when he stood up."

"He's taking *what?*"

"Viagra."

"VIAGRA?"

"Yep."

"How in the hell did he get Viagra?" Ann asked.

"His doctor gave it to him. I've been telling him he don't need that stuff at his age, but you know him—he don't listen to no one, especially me."

"Why on earth would the doctor do that?"

"I have no idea. Maybe Mr. Bill made him," Earline suggested.

"Well, he or I have to unmake him! This is ridiculous."

Ann was stunned. Another thing about her father she did *not* want to know, and now she had to call the doctor and tell him to make up some excuse for why Daddy could no longer take Viagra. Every day? What on earth was wrong with him?

Ross thought it was hilarious when Ann told him, and the rest of us just groaned and rolled our eyes. So typical of Daddy to cause everyone around him trouble by acting like a teenager.

True to her word, Ann did call the doctor, and Daddy did stop taking Viagra. He was not happy about it. He did not, however, stop looking for women. In fact, way too shortly after Pat's death, he enlisted Earline in finding some "dates" for him. He had qualifications: they had to be between forty and forty-five (remember, he was eighty-six!), "not ugly," and without diseases.

Earline got him back for dragging her into his search when she sent him on a wild goose chase to the county dump to check out a friend of hers who was the office manager. Daddy went under the guise of looking for car parts so he could give her the once over before making any formal ask. According to Earline, she did not pass the test, and Daddy came home mad as a hornet. However, he never asked her to do *that* again!

Idiot.

Daddy took his last breath with Earline at his side. In the days before his death, he thought she was Stella many times. He told her he and Shelby had to get up to go to school, talked to her as if she were Nonna, and was rarely lucid. She went right along with him, wherever he was in his mind, and never flinched at the hard stuff. He—and all of us—were so lucky to have her.

STELLA AND EARLINE WERE WITH my father at the beginning and at the end of his life. They both deserve the Medal of Honor for valor in the face of dealing with him—Stella for keeping him alive throughout his Tom Sawyerish boyhood and Earline for helping him die. Neither task was easy. Bill Boorhem was determined to live and die his way, on his own terms, in his own time, and to hell with anyone who tried to change that. These two women, however, found the key to his heart and unlocked the side of him that could be managed. Because of that, my brothers, sisters, and I are eternally grateful and forever in their debt.

The Not-So-Fun Stuff

IT WAS NOT ALL FUN and games. Dementia has a way of stripping away any sense of dignity as it strips away its victim's brain. The person you knew is no longer there, and what remains is a combination of their past, their distorted present, their current hallucinations, and their imaginary friends (or enemies). Then, suddenly, your father is back—for a brief moment—just long enough for you to hope he will stay. But he doesn't, and you are once again sucked down the rabbit hole with him back to Wonderland with all the insanity that goes with it.

Here's a perfect example. One morning, Daddy and I were sitting at the breakfast table having a nice conversation, when out of the blue, he asked, "Where's Pat?"

Dumbstruck, I tried to think of how to navigate that question. Should I lie and say she had gone to the store and hope he forgets he ever asked? Should I tell him the truth? Should I change the subject? Should I have a coughing spell and say I have to go get a cough drop and pray he forgets the question? Jesus H., *this* is what I mean when I say it was not all fun and games.

I opted for the truth: "Daddy, Pat is no longer with us."

"Whaddya mean, she's no longer with us?"

"Well, Pat died, Daddy," I said gently.

"WHAT? Nah! That can't be right! She was just here!"

"No, actually, Daddy, she wasn't. She died several years ago."

The look on his face—incredulousness, confusion, horror, anger, and sadness all mixed up together—literally broke my heart.

"Well, I don't remember that!" he said.

"I know you don't. But you will. We had a really nice funeral for her, and you were there."

"I was?" he asked.

"Yep. We all were. It was really a beautiful service."

He sat there for a really, really long time gazing out the window. Finally, he looked at me and sighed, "Well, I'll be goddamned."

After a few more minutes, he came back to the present and quietly said, "Yep, she sat right there in that goddamn chair and died."

Holding back tears, I whispered, "Yes, Daddy, she did. I knew you'd remember."

———————

ANOTHER PARTICULARLY TRAUMATIC INCIDENT OCCURRED late one night. I remember it like it was yesterday. We had eaten dinner and had a nice evening on the screen porch, and it was time for bed.

"Night, Daddy. I'm headed up to bed," I told him.

"OK. I'm going, too. Sleep tight."

"You too! Love you."

Because his room was downstairs, we kept a baby monitor on to pick up any weird goings on down there. Sometime around 2 or 3 a.m., I heard this rustling on the baby monitor. It sounded like someone was trying to smooth out a sheet or was rooting around in covers. Then I heard this creaking noise along with the rustling. *What the fuck is that?* I asked myself. After listening a bit longer, I decided I had better go check.

I walked into his bedroom and there, halfway on the floor and halfway in his swivel chair, was my father. He was on his knees and looked like he was praying, except that he was all wompy-jawed, almost turned on his back, holding onto the seat and swiveling back and forth.

"Daddy! Oh my god! Are you all right? What happened?" I asked.

"I don't know. I just know I can't get up," he said.

"OK. Well, let me help you."

Moving that man whom I called slight in other parts of this story was like trying to move a two-ton bag of cement. Total dead weight. There was no way I was going to get him up off that floor by myself.

Shit, shit, shit, I thought to myself. To Daddy, I said, "It's OK, you just rest there a minute while I think about what to do. Are you in any pain? Anything broken or hurt?"

"No, I don't think so," he replied.

I thought about my options. If I called an ambulance, it would take them at least an hour to get out here. If I called Ross, that would do nothing but upset Ross. I couldn't call Earline because she lived an hour away, too. My only option was to call Lorenzo at 3:00 a.m. and tell him I couldn't pick my father up from the floor.

"Hello?" he answered the phone.

"Lorenzo?"

"Yes," he said.

"This is Harriet, Bill's daughter, up at the farmhouse."

"Oh, yes. How can I help you?" This must not have been new to him as he acted like it was perfectly normal for him to get calls at 3:00 a.m.

"Daddy has fallen, he's half on and half off his chair, and I can't for the life of me lift him. He's stuck there unless I can get some help to get him back into bed," I told him.

"I'll be right there."

Praise God and all the angels—if Ann is going to sit at the right hand of God, surely Lorenzo will sit at his left. An angel of a man himself, he loved my dad and would have done anything for him.

Lorenzo lived in a house on the farm, so he was there in ten minutes. Strong as an ox, he picked Daddy up like he was a rag doll and got him steady on his feet.

"There you go, Mr. Bill. Be careful getting up in the night! Let someone help you next time!"

"Yeah, I will. Just help me get back in bed," Daddy requested. Lorenzo did.

I tucked Daddy in and walked Lorenzo out through the garage to thank him: "I cannot thank you enough."

"My pleasure. Call me any time. I know y'all need a lot of help with him," he said.

"You can say that again!"

Back in the house, I crawled into bed with Daddy and told him, "I'm gonna sleep with you tonight, just to be sure you're OK."

"All right."

Everything got really quiet, and just as I was starting to relax a bit, Daddy hurled the covers off the bed, jumped up, and roared, "I gotta get outta here!"

"WHAT? Daddy! What is wrong?"

"I said I gotta get outta here!" he roared again.

"Why? What's wrong?" I asked.

"I just have to get out of here!" At this, he headed toward the window by the bed and tried to open it. "Come open this goddamn window!"

"Daddy, *why*?"

"'Cause I have to leave!"

"Daddy, you can't get out that way."

"The hell I can't! Open this damn thing, or I'll break it!"

My ex-fighter pilot dad was wrestling with the window and the window shade like they were some dreaded enemy that must be slain. He had lost his fucking mind, and I was about to lose mine.

"OK, OK. Just a minute!" I said.

I went over to the window, gently moved him away to prevent him from wrestling *me*, pulled up the shade, and opened the window all the way.

"About damn time!"

At that point, he pulled down his pajama bottoms and acted like he was peeing out the window. Astonished, I just stood there agape. After a few seconds, he pulled his pants back up, turned around, and said, "OK. You can close it now."

At this point, having no idea what just happened, I was totally freaked out. But I somehow managed to ask, "Can we go back to bed now?"

"No. I have to go pee," he said.

Since this whole nightmare was so far beyond my understanding, I didn't even try to respond to that statement or talk sense into him. I just agreed and walked him into the bathroom where he once again took down his pajama bottoms and actually peed—into the toilet, thank heavens.

"You done now?" I asked.

"Yep."

"OK. Let me get you back in bed."

"OK."

We got back into bed, and he was asleep in no time. I, however, was up for the rest of what little of the night was left. I couldn't decide whether to laugh hysterically or sob uncontrollably. Either one would have been appropriate. Instead, I got up, went into the kitchen, and scarfed down a few Ding Dongs. That helped. I slept on the couch until Daddy woke up later that morning. He walked into the living room and asked, "What in the hell are you doing on the couch?" He remembered nothing of last night.

"Oh, nothing. Just got up early and decided to take a little nap till you got up," I lied.

"Oh, OK. Nice nap?"

"Of course. I've never had a bad nap."

THE NEXT TIME I WAS at the farm, Daddy was sure we were getting ready to be invaded. He insisted we get into the car and "Get the hell out of here!" Sound familiar?

I was like, "Sure thing, let's do it." Anything to keep from arguing with him or trying to tell him the war ended decades ago.

We hopped into the car and drove to the Sonic, one of his favorite haunts. He ordered black coffee—of course—and I got a hot fudge sundae, strongly believing I deserved one. We sat there quite a while and had a nice conversation, talking about all the other cars there in the drive-in, the weather, and his horses.

Finally, he said, "Let's go," and we took off. The drive back to the farm was about thirty minutes, so we spent that time looking for hawks and watching out for the highway patrol. "Do *not* go over fifty-five on this road. The cops lie in wait and *will* get you. Pat got so many tickets on this road, you'd think she'd have learned to slow the hell down, but she never did. I'm surprised she didn't end up in jail over those damn tickets."

He was one to talk! But I said nothing and stayed religiously at fifty-five mph. After a little while we arrived home.

"Here we are! All safe and sound," I announced cheerfully.

"Yeah, well, we'll be lucky to get out of here alive."

Deciding he was back in the war, I simply patted his knee, got out of the car, went around it, and opened his door. I helped him out and walked him inside through the garage. Inside I fixed him some more coffee that he drank with a big piece of chocolate cake Earline had baked, and Bill Boorhem's life, both present and past, went on.

———————

THE DAY YOU HAVE TO wrestle car keys from a fiercely independent person is not a fun day. The task of confiscating Daddy's car keys and keeping him from driving fell to Ross and Earline. Earlier in the Daddy-with-dementia journey, several incidents solidified the need to ground our father permanently. The first time, he drove to Dallas from Shreveport as he had done a thousand times before, but this time, he missed the toll road exit to his condo, and our heretofore never-been-lost-in-his-life father ended up lost at sea and totally confused in Frisco. He called Ross, and Ross was able to get him to the condo with over-the-phone directions, but it took a while. Of course, Daddy took no responsibility for getting lost—he blamed it all on construction and bad signage—and wouldn't even admit he was lost. That weekend we all went out to dinner, and Ross was kidding him about it.

"I was *not* lost," Daddy said, indignant.

"Pops, come on. You ended up in Frisco!"

"Only because of the goddamn construction on the toll road that blocked the sign to my exit."

I'm pretty sure there was no construction, but thank goodness, Ross did not share that information with Daddy.

"Y'all just leave me the hell alone. I'm fine," Daddy said.

And that was that. You did not argue with Crusher Bill. He did drive back to Shreveport without mishap, but the next incident made us all stop and think.

He and Ross were again at the condo in Dallas—I have no idea if Daddy drove himself there—and Daddy said to Ross, "This is a nice hotel."

Astonished, Ross exclaimed, "Daddy, this is your condo! This is the Bonaventure—it's your furniture, your clothes in the closet, your balcony."

Daddy looked around, and all he said was, "Huh!"

That was enough to freak us out, but the final incident was the icing on the cake. Daddy took himself to the post office in Belcher like he did every day. He got out of the car, went inside, opened his P.O. box, got out the mail, closed the P.O. box, walked back out to the car, got in, and couldn't figure out how to start it. His car was the new push-button-starter kind, but he was looking all over for his keys. I'm not exactly sure what happened next, but here is what I imagine happened: He called Earline. "Earline, I can't find my goddamn car keys."

"What do you mean, you can't find your car keys? You don't have any car keys," I imagine her replying.

"The hell I don't! How else am I gonna get this damn thing started?"

"Mr. Bill, you have to push the Start button."

"The *what?*" he would ask, incredulous.

"The *Start* button."

"You don't start a damn car with a button. Where. Are. My. Keys?"

"Stay right there. I'm coming to the post office. I'll be there in ten minutes."

"Bring my keys!"

Earline got there, started the car, and followed Daddy home. I'm sure she immediately called Ann or Ross, and they all decided it was time for Crusher Bill to give up his keys—or button.

How to make that happen was the magic question. Several times before they found a solution, Daddy would go out to his car, try to get in, and try to start it. Earline would have to talk him out of doing that with some distraction and get him back into the house. It was never a pretty scene, with lots of cussing on Daddy's part and lots of yelling and pleading on Earline's part.

Ross and Earline finally decided to hide the car in the barn and tell Daddy it was in the shop for major repairs. Out of sight, out of mind, right? No such luck. Daddy hounded them both about his car for weeks and never really forgot about it. Why in the hell his dementia didn't wipe that memory out is the $64,000 question, but it did not. He did, however, quiet down about it, and as long as someone was available to take him where he wanted to go, he was OK. So another transition in the Daddy-with-dementia journey was complete.

But it all went downhill from there.

THE DAY THAT DADDY SLAMMED Ann up against a wall and hissed, "Don't tell me what to do. I'll fucking kill you!" shit got real. She was on the phone with Ross, and Daddy was bound and determined to go see Lorenzo, who was supposedly down at the barn. Ann was hoping Ross could talk him out of it, but no luck. Daddy opened the door to go outside, Ann tried to stop him, and he lost it.

After recovering from the wall incident and with Ross still on the phone, Ann agreed to drive Daddy down to the barn. How she did that, I'll never know, and how she kept from decking him for being such a monster is a testament to her respect for him. Ross stayed on the phone throughout the entire episode in case help needed to be summoned, and with Lorenzo not being down at the barn after all, Ann drove him back to the house, and life went on.

But not really. That incident triggered regular sibling conference calls to decide what needed to happen next to keep everyone safe. Daddy's nurse told Ann earlier in the dementia journey that he could get mean and violent, and now that had happened.

Ann looped the neurologist in and was told that Daddy needed a psychiatric evaluation to be prescribed anti-anxiety meds. He also said that Daddy needed to be admitted into a geriatric psych unit for that evaluation.

Back on the phone, we all agreed that this was the best course of action, but Ann was the one who had to ultimately decide, sign all the papers, get him admitted, and explain to him what was happening. It was gut-wrenching for her. But she did it, and Daddy got the evaluation he needed.

Beth, who was working in the home healthcare industry at the time and was a lifesaver to us as we navigated the maze of dementia care, texted us the first night he was on the unit: "Well, blow my skirt up! Just talked to the charge nurse on Daddy's floor, and it appears that Daddy has made quite an entrance, as usual. He's already gone around and introduced himself to everyone on the floor, told them all about his kids, about his time in the war, about the farm and all his horses. He had a good dinner and has been Mr. Charming. Praise the Lord!"

Me: "OMG! Praise the Lord and pass the biscuits!"

Ann: "Mark off Day One as a miraculous success!"

Barbra: "Glad Daddy is not unhappy and distressed. He always DID love an audience!"

No response from Ross. He always was a little slow.

The longer he stayed on the unit, however, the more unhappy he became. After a three-week stay, Earline picked him up to go home, and as the nurse, who was *very* attractive, wheeled Daddy out the front door in a wheelchair, he asked Earline, "You think she's single? She's pretty damn cute!"

"Oh my god, Mr. Bill, stop it. You're way too old to be thinking that."

"The hell I am! I'm not dead yet! Ask her if she'll go out with me."

"I most certainly will not!"

So, Daddy, being his usual lascivious self, took it upon himself to turn around in the wheelchair, pat the nurse on her butt, and ask her out on a date.

Apoplectic, Earline profusely apologized to the nurse, who responded, "Oh, please. Not to worry. Happens all the time with our older patients."

After the nurse stunt and on the way home, Daddy said to Earline, "If I'd 'a stayed there one more day, they'd 'a killed me!"

"I wish they had! Would sure make my life a lot easier!" Earline replied.

"Well, that's not a very nice thing to say."

"Well, sometimes you're not a very nice person!" she told him.

"Well...hell."

During his hospital stay Daddy got his meds situated, and Ann got a breather to regroup. While he was in the hospital, she, Ross, and I went to look at an assisted living / memory care place in case the doctor recommended it as a next step.

That was grim.

I don't care how cheery they try to make those places and how fancy they are, they exude the aura of *this is your last stop before six feet under* from every nook and cranny. Don't get me wrong—they do great work and provide a crucial service—there's just no way to cover up the pending specter of death.

Ann was the one who was most on the front lines with Daddy, so it was really her call to keep him at home or place him in a memory care facility. None of us wanted to see his name on one of those rooms, but we were ready to back Ann in whatever she decided.

In the end, however, we didn't need it. Daddy was fairly disoriented when he got home from the hospital and didn't really know where he was, so we decided on twenty-four-hour in-home care to give him time to readjust to his environment.

He told Ann one day at lunch, while sitting at the kitchen table, "Well, this is a really nice hotel!" Sound familiar?

She corrected him, saying, "No, Daddy! This is your home!"

All he said was, "Huh."

End Days

ROSS THINKS IT WAS AFTER that hospital stay that Bill Boorhem decided he had had enough. Although he was doing better mentally, and his meds were helping his anxiety, he was pretty much done. As the weeks went on, he got quieter and quieter, started seeing things from his childhood, thought Earline was Stella, and several times thought he had to get up to go to school with his brother, Shelby. He told Earline often, "I want to go home. I'm so tired."

He kept telling Ross that he needed to get to the train station in Memphis.

"Why there, Pops?" Ross would ask.

"'Cause that's where my mother and my brother, Shelby, are. I have to meet them."

"But why?"

"Because that's where the train to heaven leaves from!"

Wow. Daddy lived in Memphis as a kid and always loved that city. I guess that's where he felt home was. He kept saying, "I just want to go home" to both Ross and Earline, and when Ross finally asked him where home was, he said, "Memphis." His heart stayed there all those years he was moving around the country, through all his adult years, and even till the very end. Every heart needs a home, I guess, and Memphis was his.

His dementia continued to progress, and the home healthcare nurse strongly recommended to Ann that we call in hospice, so we did. Toward the end, I posted a couple of updates from the farm:

"It looks like we are moving into the good-bye stages. Daddy has not been out of his room all week, is eating and drinking very little, and has expressed displeasure at his situation, i.e., 'I'm tired of this shit!' He's very quiet, resting comfortably, in no pain, and blessedly he still remembers us. Thank God for Beth. Once again, she is leading us through this latest transition. I'll keep you posted, going over again next weekend. As always, thanks for your thoughts, prayers, and good energy. I so appreciate it."

A couple of weeks later, I posted this:

"Daddy is still with us. We are in the waiting time…waiting 'til he or his body decides it's time to go home. Sister Barbra got to spend time with him this weekend, along with Ann and Ross, and I'll go next weekend if he is still with us. Very happy that we have gotten all necessary Navy discharge papers for him to have a military funeral. He is, as always, doing it his way!"

Beth was the last one of us to be with Daddy before he died. She saw him the weekend before and then called Earline on Wednesday to see how he was doing. Earline told her Daddy was having difficulty breathing and that his breathing was irregular. She thought he had died a couple of times, the space between his breaths was so long. Being in home-health care, Beth knew this was Cheyne-Stokes breathing, which happens when a person nears death.

After explaining to Earline what was happening, Beth called Barbra and told her about his breathing pattern and that the end was near. Barbra, being a nurse, immediately knew what Beth was talking about, but she also knew that it could happen quickly, or it could take a few days. It happened to be days.

Earline called Beth a second time Thursday and told her the nurse wanted to catheterize Daddy because he wasn't urinating, and Earline wanted Beth's opinion. Although he was very uncomfortable, Beth knew that grumpy old man Crusher Bill would never tolerate having a catheter shoved up his you-know-what, even at death's door. Besides, he had given strict instructions: "Don't put any of those damn tubes or needles in me to keep me alive. That's horseshit."

Consequently, Beth told the nurse that it was time to start a morphine drip to keep him comfortable and that nothing else was to be done. That's what happened, and there was no further effort to sustain his life. That was late Thursday.

Daddy died peacefully in his sleep early Friday morning. The date was May 31, 2013. He was almost ninety-one years old. On that morning, he got to go home, with Earline at his bedside, and join all those who had gone before. I'm sure it was quite a reunion.

I asked Daddy one time at the farm what he thought happened after we die.

"Hell, I don't know," he said.

"Well, do you believe in heaven and hell?" I asked.

"I don't know, but I can tell you one damn thing. If there is a hell, I'd know a lot more people there than I would in heaven!"

Always the jokester.

I hope he went to heaven if there is one. He may have known more people in hell, but he didn't belong there. Sure, he had issues, but deep down, William Boorhem was a stellar human being—brave, funny as hell, bigger-than-life, handsome, smart, and a builder of empires. He helped more people than I can count in more ways than any of us will ever know, loved life, and lived it his way. When he said, "Life is for the living," he meant it.

Forever a realist, he sat Ann down one day while he was still in the game and said, "I don't have that much longer. We need to start selling the horses and figuring out what to do with all this crap." Ann swears to me that she called me from her car sobbing on the way home from that discussion. I have absolutely no recollection of that happening at all. My way of blocking out the tragedy of his words? Who knows? But sell the horses they did, and figure out what to do with all the crap they also did. God bless Ann.

The day he died, I posted this on Facebook:

"To all my Crusher Bill fans out there: Our sweet Daddy was finally called home early this morning. He passed peacefully in his sleep with his beloved caregiver, Earline, at his side. Services will be late next week in Dallas. I'll post info and obituary when done.

What a journey this has been. 'The Year of Grace,' as I've named it, was transformative for me and I hope helpful to Daddy as we all gathered close to help. Your good wishes, thoughts, and prayers have sustained my sibs and me. I shared so many of your comments about "Crusher Bill stories" with Daddy, and he LOVED them, loved having a fan club and being famous! I'll post more info as I get it. Peace."

When Earline knew for sure that Daddy was gone, she opened all the windows and doors "so his spirit won't get trapped in the house!" I'm not sure where that came from, but she believed it, so we can breathe a sigh of relief that his spirit was set free.

After that, I'm not sure whether she called Ross or Ann first—probably Ann—and shared the news. Whom I heard it from is a total blank—I seem to be good at forgetting traumatic moments. Ann said later that she texted all of us the next morning to let us know, but I don't remember that and can't find that text. I'm sure it did happen, though, and like many other parts of my life is filed away somewhere in the cobwebs of my brain.

I remember being sad but not devastated. After all, I had the chance to spend so much time with him and get all my Daddy and Crusher Bill unfinished business finished. My grief for my father—unlike that for my mother, which was messy and complicated—was clean and simple. No loose ends. No hard feelings. Only gratitude. I had transformed our fraught and fractured relationship into one that, although not perfect, was good enough. I found a new father and a new me in relation to him.

For that I am incredibly grateful and forever changed.

The United States of America
honors the memory of

William Boorhem

This certificate is awarded by a grateful
nation in recognition of devoted and
selfless consecration to the service
of our country in the Armed Forces
of the United States.

President of the United States

Certificate from President Barak Obama honoring Daddy for his naval service.

Epilogue

THE YEAR OF GRACE WAS published on the tenth anniversary of Daddy's death. Why it took me so long to finish this book is anyone's guess, but the big things in my life have tended to happen every ten years. So I guess this is par for the course.

The funeral was as raucous as Daddy himself. We had a pianist play all his favorite '30s and '40s songs instead of hymns, and I rehashed many of the stories you just read in a too-long but hilariously poignant eulogy, which I wrote with the help of the entire Boorhem tribe. Our childhood choir director conducted the service, and we showed a fabulous video of his life created by my niece Rebecca with all the aunties hovering over her, micromanaging every step of the way. The link to the video and the eulogy are in the Appendix.

Ross may have had the best line of the day when it was his turn to speak: "So Pops came to me in a dream last night. I haven't told any of my sisters this, but he came to me and said, 'To hell with that stupid video y'all are doing. I'd much rather have a never-ending loop of Fox News!'"

Perfect.

Then there was my faux pas at the end of the eulogy when I meant to say what an impact Daddy had on so many people, and I instead said, "What an impact he had on so many women"! Realizing my gaffe, I tried to save face by saying, "Well, he *did* love women!" Not the solution. I think my carousing father was sitting on my left shoulder making me say that.

Leslie missed the whole thing due to being in Prague for a summer fellowship, so she sent a beautiful statement that we shared with everyone; it's also in the Appendix. We conference-called her right before the service to loop her in. Barbra and David flew in from Seattle; Andi, David, and their kids came from Montana; Beth and her clan drove up from Austin, as did Kat and Dan; and Wiley and Nanda flew in from California. Cousin Ray Rutherford flew in from Omaha to represent Mother's side of the family. The rest of us were local. Needless to say, the part about survivors in the obit was very long! I told you, builder of empires.

A Navy uniformed detail provided the core elements of military funeral honors: the playing of "Taps" and the folding and presentation of the United States flag. It was extremely touching and powerful—Daddy would've loved it. Being the eldest, Ann got the flag, and boy did she deserve it after all she had been through the previous five years.

The next week, we held a memorial service for him in Shreveport at the racetrack with all his horse buddies, trainers, back-side helpers, and Louisiana friends present. Ross was the main speaker for that event and did a great job sending Pops off to his next adventure.

Back in Dallas, I posted this update on Facebook:

"Home again. Crusher Bill has been memorialized, eulogized, sung for, prayed over, and laid to rest. Life goes on. Fly high, Daddy."

When I said that night, early in the year of Daddy-with-dementia, "Yep, Daddy, we'll give this thing a whirl, as long as we can!" that is exactly what we did. Each of us in our own way gave it a whirl with Daddy, helping with our talents, our expertise, our love, our stories, and our support. It was a momentous year, truly filled with grace and blessings—one that not one of us will soon forget.

William Boorhem did it his way. And although I now know that he was not immortal, he will live in my heart forever. And when I see him in my dreams, he is dancing with the angels and raising hell in heaven. And down here, Daddy, I will live life, and I will *not* waste it.

And so, The Year of Grace came to an end…sacred, sad, hilarious, joyous, transformative, and full of love.

All I can say is, what a gift.

Military flag given to Ann at Daddy's military funeral service.

Postscript

LIFE DOES, INDEED, GO ON, and all the sibs except Bill, whom we lost in 2002, are alive and well. Daddy's dementia and death impacted each of us in different ways. There's no right way to get through the journey we took with him or grieve his loss. Like Daddy, we each did it our way, helped how we could, and stuck together—that's what tribes do.

Ann

My sister Ann is reliving her teen years by traipsing all over the country with her daughters, Andi and Becca, to see her favorite country bands in concert. She has no pets, doesn't like animals—especially after having to keep Lady in her old age—and therefore plans on no pets in the future.

Daddy's dementia was harder on Ann than on anyone else. Being on the front lines with him longer than the rest of us took a huge toll. It was extremely difficult for her to watch her father, whom she adored, deteriorate and lose himself. As she told us not long ago, "Making that decision to put him into a psych hospital almost killed me, even though I knew it was the right thing to do." I don't know how she could have survived those years if she hadn't had Earline for support every day. They call themselves "sisters from different misters" to this day and stay in touch regularly.

After Daddy's death, Ann literally sat on the couch for two years recovering. We encouraged her to take all the time she needed, which she did, and which paid off handsomely because when she decided it was time to re-enter life, she went whole hog, as you can see above!

Ross

Ross loves dogs and sadly lost his soul-canine, Helen, last year. After mourning her, he now has a Morkie (Maltese and Yorkie) puppy named Hattie Hazel after our grandmother. She's darling, but since Ross did not follow my instructions on crate training, she poops wherever she likes. Weirdly, she goes outside to pee just fine—I guess she likes leaving him little nuggets of herself so he doesn't forget her. He continues to build and remodel houses, although on a limited scale, and becomes more like Crusher Bill every day. He's still my bestie, even though he's on the wrong side of politics.

Ross took being Daddy's go-to guy throughout the dementia journey in stride. Always calmer than the rest of us, it was a perfect role for him. As he told me, "My unfinished business with Pops got finished when I came out to him in rehab. Once that was over, our relationship became and stayed comfortable and enjoyable. Him blowing up my phone twenty times a day was just part of the deal, and he depended on me to be there. That was an easy gift I could give him."

Beth

Beth stays young by toting her grandkids all over here and yonder and attending every sporting and artistic event they are in. She, too, has a puppy, named Archie, whose sole job is to keep her husband, O.E., happy and occupied. He's doing a great job of that and is cute as a button. I'm not usually into shih tzus, but he's a keeper. She sends photos of him from Austin regularly for us to *ooh* and *aah* over, and since there are six of us in all— more if you add Lyndsey and any of the grandkids—one text message can generate a day-long text string that would drive a saint crazy. And of course, they always happen when I'm trying to nap. Quite annoying.

The hardest things for Beth about Daddy's dementia were the geographic distance between Austin and Shreveport and the fact that her ability to visit was limited by her husband's health problems. She was the resident home healthcare and dementia expert whom we turned to time and time again as we made decisions along the way. She told us, "I was really happy that I had the knowledge to help, but let me tell you, it sucked weenies!"

Barbra

Barbra is the only one who continually bitches about 'being old,' with the rest of us cemented firmly in denial and fighting 'the alternative' every step of the way. After her husband, David, died, we moved her and her two dogs back to Dallas from Maui on a private jet, no less, because it was during COVID and regular airlines wouldn't ship her dogs. No comment there, except to say that flying in that posh jet was *so* much fun—especially since Barbra paid for it!

However, the house that Ross remodeled for her was not ready, so she and her two dogs stayed with me and my two dogs for a month while Ross took his sweet time, as usual, to finish the house. *That* was fun. We had to keep the dogs separate for fear of war, so our lives were scheduled by texts to each other from our bedrooms around when each pair of dogs could be out in the common areas. Her dog, Chase, took over my couch and the fuzzy blanket on it to the point that Barbra had to buy one just like it for him at the new house so he'd quit pouting. But she and I got along fine, and the house was finally finished. We landed in Dallas on November 1, and she moved into her house in mid-December.

Barbra was the farthest away, being in Seattle and then Hawaii, during the dementia journey. As a nurse and a pragmatist, she knew what to expect as the dementia progressed, so she felt somewhat removed from the whole process. However, she stayed in the loop with all of us and helped us understand what was coming next when we had all those conference calls. She made it to the farm twice to spend time with Daddy, and the first time she was there, she texted all of us: "Well it's a miracle. Daddy and I have only told each other to 'get fucked' once!"

Kevin

Kevin and his wife, Lyndsey, spend every free minute attending their extremely athletic daughter's soccer and softball practices, games, and tournaments. Her name is Landry—get it, Tom Landry?—so how could she not be a star? I fully expect to see her playing football in my lifetime. They have two very large pitties who are as gentle as lambs, and Kevin and Lyndsey, like most of the rest of us, love animals. Ann is the only outlier, and we have no idea what happened to her.

Kevin loved the farm, horse racing, and everything connected to Foxwood. He and Lyndsey wanted to move to the farm eventually, but when he lost his mom, Pat, and then Daddy, that dream was not to be. That was hard enough, but the worst thing for Kevin was that Landry missed out on knowing Pat and Popio and the farm. I know what that's like, and it really hurts.

Harriet

I retired from the nonprofit I was running and, at the behest of Ross, sold my hundred-year-old money pit of a house and let him totally remodel a midcentury modern abode for me. I absolutely love it! Soon after moving into the new house, I lost my big golden retriever, Tucker, close to his fourteenth birthday and mourned him for a year before I brought Luna, another golden retriever, home from Arkansas. The next year I drove to Michigan in the dead heat of summer (can you say cray cray?) to pick up my long-coated German shepherd, Kora, and added her to the family. Tallulah, the Maine Coon cat, is the latest animal to join the family, having joined in April of this year.

Two years after Daddy's death, a friend and colleague of mine and I created a leadership development program called It's Lonely at the Top! for women who run nonprofits. It's been great fun and has given me the opportunity to use everything I learned in the trenches to help other women.

In my spare time, I walk my dogs, sit by the pool, watch British TV, live for yoga, get my hair colored and highlighted, and get my nails and toes done—all necessities to stay forever young.

The Boorhem Tribe Now

Harriet with daughters Leslie (L) and Kat (R). Photo courtesy of Leslie Boorhem-Stephenson.

Harriet with daughters Leslie (L), Kat (R), and Kat's husband, Dan. Photo courtesy of Leslie Boorhem-Stephenson.

Ann's daughter, Andrea, and her family. L-R: Luke, Andrea, David (Andrea's husband), Bailey, Jacob (Bailey's boyfriend). Photo courtesy of Leslie Boorhem-Stephenson.

Ann with daughter Andrea's family. L-R: Luke, Andrea, David, Ann, Bailey, Jacob. Photo courtesy of Leslie Boorhem-Stephenson.

Ann's daughter, Rebecca, and her son, Sebastian. Photo courtesy of Leslie Boorhem-Stephenson.

Ann with her daughter, Rebecca, and Rebecca's son, Sebastian. Photo courtesy of Leslie Boorhem-Stephenson.

Kevin with his wife, Lindsay, and daughter, Landry. Photo courtesy of Leslie Boorhem-Stephenson.

The girls! Older, but still forever young at heart! L-R: Ann, Harriet, Barbra, and Beth. Photo courtesy of Leslie Boorhem-Stephenson.

Brother Bill's youngest son, Noah, and his wife, Alma, with their new baby, Emelia. Photo courtesy of Leslie Boorhem-Stephenson.

Brother Bill's oldest son, Wiley, with his wife, Fernanda, and their two kids, William and Beatrice.

Beth's daughter, Sarah Jane, with her husband, David, and their kids, Will and Jane.

Brother Ross—looking handsome, as always!

Beth and Barbra, the twins, looking twinsie!

Beth's kids, Bub and Sarah Jane. We lost Bub tragically in October of 1998.

Beth with her husband, O.E.; daughter, Sarah Jane; son-in-law, David; and grandkids, Will and Jane.

Beth with her husband, O.E. Their entire family are rabid Texas Longhorn fans.

Texas fans David, Jane, Sarah Jane, and Will—Beth's family—at a UT football game.

Ross with his new puppy, Hattie, 2022.

THROUGHOUT THE LAST TEN YEARS, I've stabbed at writing this book many times, only to get distracted by the first shiny thing I saw. Now that it's finally finished, I have no idea what I will do with my time. Stay tuned.

Overall, we are each happy, grateful for another day, and missing our dad. He left a huge hole when he exited, and my writing this book was most likely an attempt to fill that void.

Ross and Ann are still in close touch with Earline, and she and her girls regularly attend big family events. I often wonder if Main Street Café still has its shrine to Foxwood and the horses. I also wonder if that waitress in Vivian ever got her teeth fixed.

Grace to you all, and peace out.
XXOO,
Harriet

P.S. HE KEPT ME IN THE WILL!

Acknowledgments

RAISE YOUR GLASSES WITH ME for a toast to Ann Medlin and Ross Boorhem for shouldering the heaviest load during the Daddy-with-dementia era. I am acutely aware that, if not for them, my time with Daddy could have been much more difficult and much less amenable to writing a book about. They were in the trenches long before I was and dealt with the "not-so-fun stuff" for several years before I came into the rotation. I owe a huge debt of gratitude to both.

The rest of my tribe deserves huge kudos also, as fact-checkers, readers, encouragers, storytellers, and participants in *The Year of Grace*. I'm grateful they didn't shy away from the not-so-pleasant memories I shared and didn't murder me for telling the story from my perspective. After all, when you have six kids and one step-kid, you have seven different interpretations of family events that many times conflict with one another. The fact they didn't censor my take on our family deserves high praise.

I'm deeply grateful to my business partner, Tanya McDonald, for being all things It's Lonely at the Top! for a complete summer to allow me to finish this book. I'm also grateful to the women of It's Lonely at the Top! for giving me the time and space to finish.

My daughters, Kat and Leslie, were my sounding board, my initial editors, my cheering squad, and my best critics. Honest to a fault, they kept me on the straight and narrow and on my toes throughout this journey.

Tanya, my business partner and bestie, and I hard at work on It's Lonely at the Top! stuff.

Thank you, also, to Pat Berger Stone for introducing me to Ella Ritchie, founder of Stellar Communications Houston, who served not only as my editor and publisher, but more importantly as my guide, therapist (at times), mentor, and friend. Being a total newbie to this book-writing business, I would have been a dismal failure without her expertise and help.

Earline deserves special thanks and gratitude for her undying loyalty to and love for Daddy. No one could handle him like she could. She was with him every step of the way and bore it all with humor and aplomb. Such a treasure.

Finally, I am most grateful to my father for living a life worth writing about. Although gone ten years, I can hear his voice, see his piercing blue eyes, and feel his gruffness as clearly as if he were sitting here beside me.

Although he and I were often at cross purposes, that is water way under the bridge. The Year of Grace was just that. I am so grateful for that year, for him, for the family he built, for me getting to be part of his zoom-zoom life, for the stories and memories that will be passed down through the generations, and for him giving me such great material to share with you.

I hope it brought him to life and gave you a sense of how lucky I was to be his daughter.

Daddy, age 90, dressed up for a racetrack party—handsome to the end.

Appendix

CRUSHER BILL QUOTES

"Dumbass!"
Crusher Bill's all-purpose, default expression. Also used upon arriving at the scene of a wreck caused by sixteen-year-old me slamming into a parked car with my brand-new car while trying to light a cigarette as I turned a corner with six other girls in the car with me. Please note he did not say: "You OK? Is everyone OK? Anyone else hurt?"

"Don't be a dumbass!"
Slightly more instructive.

"So, besides that, Mrs. Lincoln, how was the play?"
Any time we told him about something bad that happened to us.

"No one's gonna toot your horn for you but you!"
Advice given almost every night at the dinner table.

"My mother was tighter than copper on a penny."
On his mother. And was she ever! One summer when we stayed with her, she made us turn our underwear inside-out and wear them again before she would wash them!

"She was a looker, but she couldn't spell shit if she was standing in it!"
On his grandmother. (She was really beautiful, as her picture shows.)

"10% of the people run the world, and the other 90% don't know shit. Don't be part of the 90%!"
Frequent dinner-table advice.

"It's colder than a well-digger's butt!"
Describing winter at the Rock Crusher.

"It's colder than a witch's tit!"
Also describing winter at the Rock Crusher.

"Thousands of people have done what you're fixin' to. You're way smarter than them. So if they did it, you can, too!"
Pep talk, Crusher Bill style.

"Don't live a life of liquidation!"
His financial advice mantra.

"I'm gonna be DEAD before you finish that goddamn thing!"
After asking if I'd finished my dissertation.

"Nice of you to finish while I'm still ALIVE!"
At my doctoral graduation: Crusher Bill code for saying he was proud of me.

"My mother could talk the arm off a slot machine!"
Describing his mother. No one wanted to get cornered by her because she would hold on to your wrist, rubbing her thumb up and down your forearm whilst talking politics!

"As different as my mother and father were, they really loved each other and helped each other. My mother handled all the money. She wouldn't even let God handle the money."
Also describing his mother and hinting at how much of a control freak she was, especially about money.

"The things you own, own you."
On possessions.

"She's got champagne taste on a beer budget!"
Judging who-knows-who about living above her means.

"My mother would run anything, including the Republican Party!"
Regarding his mother, who did, literally, run the Republican Party in Arkansas.

"Hell no!"
Just to add emphasis when his answer was "No," which was frequent.

"Hey now!"
In response to anything he disagreed with. Actually, in response to anyone who disagreed with him period or didn't act right.

"Why the HELL would you want to volunteer for something when you could get paid for doing the same damn thing?"
A capitalist to the end.

"Income has to exceed outgo!"
More Crusher Bill financial wisdom.

"A man never got rich by spending all his money."
And yet even more financial advice, Crusher Bill style.

"If that horse went any slower, he'd be going backwards!"
Bemoaning any horse he bet on that wasn't going fast enough for him.

"Just look around at all that land. You OWE for every goddamn acre of it!"
To Pat about Foxwood, which he bought without the two investors who bailed on him. What he did not say: "Isn't it beautiful?" or "Aren't we lucky to have such a beautiful home?"

WILLIAM BOORHEM
June 18, 1922–May 31, 2013

View the video "Turning the Pages of His Life":

https://youtu.be/rZ6rcmTaHU4

WE PASSED IN A DREAM

An article written by Leslie Boorhem-Stephenson

As a photojournalist our job is to tell stories with images, not words. I will be the first person to hate on photographers using other people's art to promote their own but this is honestly too powerful for me not to use.

I just found out that my larger than life grandfather died back home. He was almost 91 and had lived one of the fullest lives anyone on Earth could claim. He was a fighter pilot in World War II, came home and built a business from the ground up, had a huge bustling family and finally became one of the most prestigious thoroughbred horse breeders in Louisiana. Bill Boorhem was a giant. But to me he was Popio, the kind of man that was rough around the edges, swore shamelessly but would run a thousand miles if he thought he could help. His legacy of "life is for the living" drives me to continue pursuing my dream of becoming a photojournalist.

The words in this photo, translated to English read: "We passed in a dream." In many ways I take after my grandfather's pragmatism and his skepticism of the ethereal. My closest contact with anything close to supernatural was my imaginary friend Olivia, whom I sent to boarding school after I grew bored of her at age 5 or 6. But the night of May 31st, the night/morning Popio passed, I dreamt of him.

It was one of those dreams where you are not quite fully asleep and where it is very difficult to distinguish reality from unconsciousness. I was standing at the location of my high school graduation but no one was there. I began to look around and I saw someone standing at the top of the exterior auditorium stairs and as I grew nearer I could see that it was my Popio. He wasn't the hunched, slender man that was actually at my high school graduation but the plump, red cheeked, boisterous one of my childhood. As I reached the top of the stairs I could go no further. He looked at me, gave me that big jowl-y, Boorhem grin as if he knew something I did not, turned and strode away. I awoke immediately, abruptly and covered in sweat but with the strangest sense of serenity.

If you think I am making all of this up, I will not fault you. If you think this was just my brain trying to comprehend the imminent loss of a pillar of my life, I would not find it hard to agree. What makes me begin to question every ounce of skepticism in my body is the complete calm that I felt upon waking. That is a calm I have not felt in years. And whether I am becoming a quack or not, I choose to believe that his soul felt the turbulence in mine and saw to it that I did not fear for him in his passing. We truly did pass in a dream, Popio. I thank you and will hold your contented smile in my mind's eye until we meet again.

EULOGY FOR WILLIAM BOORHEM

Good Morning / Afternoon. I am Harriet Boorhem, the youngest of the Boorhem daughters. I am greatly honored to represent the Boorhem-Hamlin family today. On behalf of my brothers and sisters and their spouses, our children and their spouses, and their children, I wish to thank each of you for joining with us in our sorrow and in our celebration of Daddy's life.

As the scribe of the family, I've written lots about Daddy: his larger-than-life personality, the escapades of his life, his unbelievable luck. There is one thing, however, about which I have never written, and today, I have a confession. Since I was a little girl, there has been part of me that believed that Daddy was immortal, that he would actually beat the odds (and if anyone could, it would be him!) and live forever.

Although we all know that can never be true, my magical thinking was not without logic. Daddy was never sick a day in his life. He started every morning whistling the revelry call down the hall, and basically lived each day *full out* as if it was his last. When most people his age started winding down, he was just revving up. He and my stepmother, Pat, started breeding and racing thoroughbreds when he was sixty-five. For the next twenty years he blew the dust off of all of us as he zoomed by, exuding more energy than all of his kids combined.

But five years ago, my stepmother died suddenly and unexpectedly. That was a terrible blow to all of us, but especially to Daddy. As always, however, he rallied and continued with his life (with a lot of help from my sister Ann and brother Ross). His motto has always been, "Life is for the living." And, so, he continued to live. But he was never the same…and so, the dismantling of my magical thinking began.

When Ross called me to say I needed to get in the rotation of helping care for Daddy—that he could no longer stay by himself—I could no longer pretend that he would live forever. Thus began what I call the "Year of Grace": the year of sacred conversations, fabulous stories told and retold, adventures in Dining Out with Daddy, "Here Kitty, Kitty" stories (more on that later), the coming together of my siblings and me for the purpose of serving our father in the best way possible, of hilarious stories of Daddy-with-dementia, of sad and painful stories of Daddy-with-dementia, of the creation of new maladies, i.e., Post Traumatic Foxwood Disorder, which included symptoms of homicidal tendencies toward Daddy, guilt for feeling homicidal, uncontrollable laughter at the crazy happenings at the farm, and the need to crawl under the covers and hide from the world for days at a time after leaving the farm. We all suffered from this from time to time, but we think we might have to commit Ann in order for her to have a full recovery—she was in the trenches the longest.

So, who *was* Bill Boorhem, aka Crusher Bill, aka Popio, aka Daddy? Well, born June 18, 1922 as the youngest son of Lillian and Shelby Boorhem, Daddy came into this life as a mischievous "Tom Sawyer" and never changed. Although a slight man, he was bigger than life with his booming voice, his gregarious personality, his love of people, and most of all, his love of an audience!

Born in Los Angeles, California, Daddy traveled with his family during the 1920s and '30s all up and down the Mississippi River following civil engineering projects that his father oversaw. He attended at least fourteen schools growing up, and when asked what the worst thing about that was, he would answer, "Having to fight my way into *every* school."

Daddy worshipped his father and followed closely in his footsteps. Although he thought his older brother, Shelby, was "the smart one," our father was a brilliant self-made businessman, leaving his children, grandchildren, and great-grandchildren an incredible safety net and legacy.

Daddy's family moved to Malvern, Arkansas from Memphis, Tennessee his junior year in high school, and it was there that he met the first love of his life, Jane McCormack. High school sweethearts, they persevered through WWII and were married on August 27, 1945. Six children followed in quick succession, and when I asked him if they had planned to have that many children, Daddy replied, "Probably not, but what else was there to do in Malvern, Arkansas?"

A naval fighter pilot in WWII, Daddy flew bombers as well as fighter planes in the South Pacific theater. Surviving being shot down twice over the Pacific, he summed up the experience of having to land the plane in the "drink" as "Nothin'" compared to being on the rescue submarine for a week—he was claustrophobic!

Upon completing his tour of duty in WWII, Daddy went straight to California and partied for two weeks before going home to Arkansas (which his mother knew nothing about). When she picked him up at the airport in Little Rock, the first thing she said was, "You look horrible! What happened?" Daddy, who was sporting a two-week hangover, said, "Well, this is just what being in the war does to you...", at which time his mother burst out crying for her poor baby! We told you...Tom Sawyer.

Daddy stayed in the Naval Reserves after WWII, flying fighter planes on training missions. On one mission, as they were flying planes from the East Coast to the Naval Air Station in Grand Prairie, Daddy decided to "visit" his family in Malvern. As eight fighter planes flew over Little Rock, he issued the order that he was taking the lead and headed up the pack that "buzzed" Pine Bluff Street in Malvern, Arkansas. They were close enough to the ground to see our mother, Jane, and twins Beth and Barbra in the front yard! Daddy's response: "Yeah, we got lots of press over that...and none of it good!"

Other escapades included him and five other fighter pilots flying planes *under* the Golden Gate Bridge several times. When I asked him if they got in trouble Daddy said, "Well, it depends on how serious a near court-martial is to you! But, we came out OK." I asked, "Was it worth it?" Daddy: "Oh, yeah."

After WWII, Daddy moved his family to Dallas in 1953 and began working for a concrete and limestone company. Here he met his future business partner and best friend, John Van Amburgh. Neither one being very good at taking orders, they were unceremoniously fired from said company. Daddy's comment about this was, "We had two wives, ten kids, and one paycheck between us." Both families somehow survived, and Daddy and John founded Crushers, Inc. (thus his nickname), a highly successful limestone-crushing company on Lake Texoma. Daddy was the operations guy and John was the sales and "dynamite" guy. It would take a book to recount their adventures, but suffice it to say, they had a good time, and their children have stories galore!

Daddy moved his family again in 1963, this time to Sherman, Texas, to be close to Crushers, Inc., where he became an active member in the business community. He served on the Boards of Directors of the Merchants and Planters National Bank and Grayson County Community College, was a member of the Chamber of Commerce and attended more high school plays, musicals, football games, and graduations than he ever cared to admit.

Upon selling Crushers, Inc. to Vulcan Materials, Daddy and Mother spent a short time in Atlanta, Georgia, with Daddy working for Vulcan. However, always the entrepreneur, Daddy couldn't stay working for someone else for long and soon returned to Sherman to start another successful aggregate company, Boorhem-Fields, with friend Joe Fields. After several years, they sold it to an Irish conglomerate, Old Castle, Inc., and Daddy fulfilled a life-long dream of breeding and racing thoroughbreds.

After the death of our mother, Daddy married the second love of his life, Pat Hamlin, in 1982. Together they built Foxwood Plantation, a beautiful and successful thoroughbred racehorse breeding farm in Belcher, Louisiana. Named "Louisiana Breeder of the Year" nine years in a row, Foxwood not only bred horses for sale, but bred many successful race horses, including Zarb's Magic, who ran in the Kentucky Derby. Daddy and Pat were deeply involved in the Backside Benevolent Association, part of the Louisiana Horse Breeders' Benevolent and Protective Association, which raises funds to support the Winner's Circle Ministry, as well as funds to support and assist backside track employees. Daddy and Pat greatly enjoyed entertaining their many friends over the years in their suite at Louisiana Downs.

So for those of us who knew Daddy, I think we will agree that the best way to show the essence of him is through his famous sayings and quotes. Sayings such as:

"No one's gonna toot your horn for you, except you!" (every night at the dinner table).

"Well I'll be g-damned!" (100 times a day).

"My mother was tighter than copper on a penny."

"10% of the world's population runs things, and the other 90% wonders what happened. Don't be part of the 90%!" (also every night at the dinner table).

"You know what they say, The rich get richer and the poor have babies" (I still don't understand this one).

"Dumbass!" (any time any of us did anything he didn't like or agree with). My most memorable turn at experiencing the "Dumbass" quote came on my sixteenth birthday when five of my best friends and I got into my brand new 1966 Chevy Impala to go for a spin. Those were the days of cigarette lighters in cars, and of course, we all smoked. So, as I bent down to light my cigarette while turning a corner (going way too fast), I ran smack dab into a *parked* car. Daddy showed up, looked at my car, looked at the parked car, looked at all six of us girls standing there crying—this is when most parents would say, "Are you all right? Anyone hurt?"—and says, "DUMBASS!"—and walked into the house to talk to the victimized neighbor.

During the Year of Grace, I decided to ask Daddy everything about his life I ever wanted to know and write down what he said.

I'd like to share some snippets of the conversations we had over the past year with you now and say that these conversations were transformative for me. I also felt many times that I was his "straight man," falling into his traps over and over. But, I got to know my father on a whole new level, and I think you will see his true humanness shining through.

———————

So, I've divided these into several categories. The first is:

"Adventures in Dining Out with Daddy"

One night we go to dinner at this horrible restaurant in Vivian that Daddy loved. The waitress comes up and asks, "Can I get y'all somethin' to drink?"

Daddy: "Iced tea."

Waitress: "Sweet or unsweet?"

Daddy: "Darlin', if I ordered sweet tea, they would have to arrest me, 'cause I would be sweeter than the law would allow!"

Getting in the car that same night, I notice Daddy is following me. "You have to get in on the other side, Daddy."

Daddy: "I know that! I'm trying to open your damn door, so you can get your ass in the car!"

Chivalry…Crusher Bill style!

———————

That night when we got home from dinner: "Well, you're a pretty darn good chauffeur." (Remember this!)

Me: "Yep, glad we made it back…"

Daddy: "Me too. I just hope it's the right place!"

———————

After dinner last night, Daddy decides he needs to call Ann. "Ann? What are you doing?"

Ann: garbled response.

Daddy: "Oh yeah. We just got back from dinner. Had roast beef, mashed potatoes, green beans…" HUH? (He had catfish.) "You want to say hello to your sister?"

Me: "Hey, Sweetie."

Ann: "Roast beef? I don't remember seeing that on the menu!"

Me: "It's not."

Loud laughter on the other end. "Well, GOOD LUCK!"

Me: "Thanks a lot."

———————

One night I've asked Daddy for his credit card, paid the bill, and given him back his card. He sees me holding the bill.

Daddy: "Did we pay the bill?"

Me: "Yep, I took care of it."

Daddy: "Well, you didn't have to pay for dinner!"

Me: "I used *your* credit card!"

Daddy: "Well I'll be g-damned!"

———————

So one night I couldn't get Daddy to eat anything at dinner, so I fixed me a BLT, and Daddy ate some chocolate pie and then immediately crashed. He just woke up wanting to know where we're going for dinner. When I said nowhere, that I'd fix him something here, he was *not* happy. I asked him if he had any good dreams during his nap… "Well, I *must* have dreamed I was *eating*!"

———————

Daddy: "How much is the bill?"

Me: "$35."

Daddy: "WHAT? For two little sandwiches?"

Me: "No…you had a cheeseburger and I had fried shrimp (delicious, BTW). My shrimp was $15, your burger was $8, then drinks, salad, etc."

Daddy: "Did you do that on purpose?"

Me: "What?"

Daddy: "Order the most expensive thing on the menu."

Me: "Of course I did (*not*). I just love to hear you be so or-nery, and gripe about it all the way home." (Thirty seconds later.)

Daddy: "How much was the bill? #%^*+}=@&$!"

Aaaannnddd we start all over again.

After paying the dinner bill, I give Daddy back his credit card. He pulls out his wallet, we put the card back, then he can't remember what to do with his wallet.

Me: "Well, it was in your back pocket. So you can put it back in."

Daddy: "That's what she said..." (as he chuckles).

OMG!

The Next Category is: "HUH?"

Me: "Daddy, put your seat belt on."

Daddy: "Oh, hell. If you weren't such a bad driver, I wouldn't need a damn seatbelt!"

Keep up...it changes like the weather! Lol.

Talking about Daddy's very musical family on his mother's side: "My grandfather was a professional musician, conductor of the Chicago Symphony...*very* highly educated. Funny thing, though...his wife couldn't spell shit if she was standing in it!"

Lordy, Lordy.

First Crusher Bill quote of the day:

"Where are the towels (kitchen)?"

Me (getting one out of a drawer): "Here you go."
Daddy: "Hell, you know your way around here!"
Me: "Yep."
Daddy: "That's *bad* news."

———————

So, Daddy says when Ross leaves: "I didn't know he was leaving so soon [he's been here three days]. Is he coming back tomorrow?"

Me: "Nope...he has to work. But I'm here, and I'm your favorite child."

Daddy: "That may be, but you're not my favorite *worker*!" (Ross cooked for him for three days...I don't cook!)

———————

So Daddy, after visiting with Leslie, says to me, "I think that's the first time I've seen your daughter."

Me: "No, you've seen her before."

Daddy: "When?"

Me: "Well, you saw her last Christmas at my house."

Daddy: "Well hell, there were so many people there, you couldn't tell who was who!"

Me: "That's true."

Daddy: "She doesn't say much about the character of your genes."

Me: "Huh?"

Daddy: "She doesn't look like you."

Me: "Well, she does look a lot like her dad."

Daddy: "Which one was he?"

Why do I listen to this crap? Lol.

———————

Ross: "Daddy's going to the barbershop tomorrow."
Me: "OK..."

Daddy: "Why do I need to go to the barbershop?"

Ross: "Well, you're looking a little nappy. Pat would turn over in her grave if she saw you!"

Daddy: "No she wouldn't. She'd be glad that I had gotten ugly, so no one else would want me!"

———————

Me: "Daddy, I found your long pajama bottoms. Wanna change?" (Daddy starts putting them on over his shorty pajama pants and boxers.)

Me: "Don't you want to take off your other ones?"

Daddy: "Why?"

Me: "'Cause you'll have on *three* pairs of pants!"

Daddy: "What's wrong with three pairs of pants?"

Me: "N-O-T-H-I-N-G."

Daddy: "That's what I thought."

HELP! Lol.

———————

Talking on the phone to my brother, Ross, one morning about the weekend.

Me: "He's done pretty well this weekend. Seems pretty perky and with it. He did, however, call you Rodney. Wanted to know when Rodney was coming back."

Ross: "Rodney? Where did he get *that*?"

Me: "No idea."

Ross: "Well, I'll be there next weekend...with my *name tag* on!"

———————

Me: "Maybe I'll see some deer on the way back to the farm."

Daddy: "You'd like to have some beer?"

Lord help me.

———————

This is one of those "Here Kitty, Kitty stories." Daddy had Zac the cat...my nemesis. The damn cat would get out, and then Daddy would obsessively call "Here kitty, kitty," insist on going outside to look for him, no matter time of day or night. So one day the lawn guys were cutting the yard, and Daddy's worried about the cat being outside.

Me: "I'm sure he's inside somewhere."

Daddy: "You don't know that. They'll chop him in half with those g-damned lawnmowers. I'm going to go outside to look for him."

Me (to myself—I'm going to chop that stupid cat in half *myself*): "Daddy, let me check your room first."

Daddy: "He never goes in there..."

I open his bedroom and out comes the idiotic cat.

Me: "Here he is, Daddy."

Daddy: "OK."

Five minutes later.

Daddy: "Where's the cat?"

%^*++=#@&$!

———————

The Last Category is: AWWWWW!

I was showing Daddy a picture of Pat's grandbaby, Landry, the daughter of my stepbrother Kevin and his wife Lindsey. Landry had just turned ten months old and was the cutest, squishiest baby you've ever seen. He looked at her a long time and said, "I can't believe Pat isn't here to see this baby. She would have been so happy to know her."

———————

Me: "Daddy, it's 10:00...you wanna get up?"

Daddy: "Hell no."

Me: "OK, when you get up, I'll fix us a BIG breakfast."

Daddy: "Sounds good. I'll dream about it!" Lol.

———————

Bittersweet day with Popio today. Moving very slowly, slept a lot, had a hard time finding words, and got really frustrated that he "slept" through dinner. But when I asked if he was ready for bed, his answer: "No, let's talk a while longer."

And that is exactly what we did!

———————

Me: "Daddy, it's bedtime, especially if we're gonna get up and go into town."

Daddy: "OK, so you're gonna go to bed, get up around 8:00 and wake me up, and we're gonna go into town."

Me: "Yep, that's correct."

Daddy: "Well, OK. Then we'll give it a whirl."

To myself: "Yep, Daddy, we'll give this thing a whirl, as long as we can!"

———————

As you can imagine, I could go on all day. Seriously, I could. (How much time do you have?) Having to choose which stories and escapades to share has been really difficult. There are just *so many*!

Like the time we were all at the dinner tables (there were so many of us, we had two tables), and Daddy asked Ross to pass the butter. Well, we always had this funny saying, "Lob or bullet?" So Ross asked, "Lob or bullet?" and Daddy said, "BULLET!" And Ross *threw* the butter dish with butter in it from one side of the kitchen to the other, barely missing Mother. Needless to say, Ross was not able to finish his dinner with us. Notice, however, that Daddy was not held responsible *at all*.

Or the adventures with the many boats that were owned by Daddy and John Van Amburgh...each one named *The Jody/Jane* after our mothers (I'm not sure I would have been happy about that if I were they). I remember at least five of them: one caught fire, one bit the dust due to dry rot, I think John probably sank two of them (forgot to put the drain plug back in), and I know for sure that Daddy ran at least one of them over tree stumps in Lake Catherine or Lake Dallas. Speaking of which, skiing behind the boat with Daddy at the helm could be a truly harrowing experience. For one thing, you could not get back in the boat till you got up on skis. Second, you had to listen to his incessant, "Keep your butt down! Let the boat pull you up!" Third, you *always* had to be on guard that if you went outside the wake, he would turn the boat in toward you, making the rope slack, and then catapulting you in the air when the boat straightened out. Last, if and when you did venture outside the wake, you had better be ready to end up going sixty miles an hour as Daddy gunned the motor in a turn that sent you flying out far to the side—I remember one time turning at least three cartwheels *on top* of the water before landing flat on my back after falling in one of those turns—it's a miracle any of us lived...and then, of course, he would turn in toward you. Fun, fun.

And then there were the snow ski trips...the one I'm thinking of in particular was especially fun with all of us piled into an antique RV driving up to Taos in a white-out snow storm. The fact that we did not drive off that mountain is purely a miracle. We literally could not see a foot in front of us. That was also the year that Ann almost skied off the mountain, Ross got the nick-name The Yellow Peril (he had on a yellow jump suit that made him look like the Abominable Snow Man), and I decided to *never* darken the likes of ski slopes ever again in my life.

On other trips when we all went, we often took two cars, and my anxiety level was through the roof the entire time. In the first place, Daddy was, of course, the lead car, and *no one* could keep up with him. In the second place, Barbra was *always* in the floorboard terrified that we would drive off some mountain road going eighty mph (not far from the truth), oh, and getting car sick. (Speaking of which, there was the time we were driving to Malvern late at night—no A/C, so we drove when it was cooler—and we *all* got sick to the tune of Bill hanging his head out of the station wagon puking his guts out. See, I told you...one story just leads to another. We may be here for a week!) It was always a toss-up which car you wanted to be in—did you want to die driving off the mountain or from second-hand smoke from Mother madly smoking to assuage *her* terror, or did you want to die listening to Brother Bill cuss Daddy to the moon and back while running red lights, passing in no-passing zones, and speeding like crazy just to keep up?

Then, there was the infamous sixtieth birthday party celebration at the pool in Farmers Branch. Ross, in all his great wisdom, thought it would be perfectly appropriate to invite a stripper to the party with a gazillion under-aged kids in the pool. Andrea, always the mothering cousin, was mortified and kept trying to cover up Sarah's eyes...I'm sure unsuccessfully. I don't think any of us knew what was happening and were so in shock, we were just kind of stuck in place! I don't even remember seeing Pat—she may have fled the scene, and I have no recollection of how it ended. What I'm sure of, however, is that Daddy had a good time.

And then the infamous Seventieth Birthday Celebration at which I thought it appropriate to dye my hair red, wear a very short sparkly dress, and sing Daddy's favorite big band tunes to him and the crowd. WHAT WAS I THINKING? In the one picture I have of Daddy and me standing up in front, he looks rather mortified. Barbra did join me at the end to help out, but she looked better than I did, so that just made things worse!

Lest you think it was all fun and games, let me set you straight. Bill Boorhem was a tough cookie to live with. He could be rigid, closed-minded, obnoxious, angry, loud, and terrifying. He and Brother Bill went at it so many times, I'm surprised they didn't kill each other. Barbra was not immune to his wrath, either (she and Bill were the "rebels" of the family); Ann was perfect; Beth and I snuck around behind his back and did most everything we wanted; and Ross was, well…Ross. We all, however, at one time or another faced his wrath, his freezeouts, his rants, being grounded for weeks at a time, being "disowned" (Bill and me), and being obliged to beg him for money. He expected nothing but the best, was furious if we made less than straight A's, and was generally uncompromising on most issues.

He was, however, also hilarious, gregarious (he never met a stranger), handsome, a lover of music and dancing (and yes, all the girls learned to dance standing on his feet—watching him and Mother dance was entrancing), *totally* engaged in life, insatiably curious, a softie if you approached him just the right way (he could never say no to Beth—what was *that* about?), fun, a fantastic story and joke teller (even if most of them were totally inappropriate), and a good soul. He bailed more folks out of jail than I can count, helped finance school for many an employee's children, loaned all of us money at one time or another, and I don't know about the rest of my sibs, but most of it I never paid back!

Last, and certainly not least, Daddy *loved* the USA. Unabashedly patriotic, one of his most famous sayings to us was, "If you ever leave American soil, you better be damned sure you have a round-trip ticket!" He was proud to have served his country, loved his years in the Navy, loved flying and being in the thick of things. He would not tolerate *any* criticism of this country, unless, of course, it was aimed at the Democratic Party.

There are many people to thank for helping to care for Daddy in the last years of his life. Earline, beloved housekeeper and caregiver, will sit at the right hand of God for her loving care and loyalty to our dad and our family. Daddy loved and trusted her completely. J.J., our "night man," gets the Boorhem Purple Heart for being the most cussed-at helper and the one who walked the floor or sat up with Daddy many a night. Lorenzo, our very own Horse Whisperer, deserves our undying gratitude for his unwavering loyalty to Daddy and to Foxwood. Although he also got cussed at (come to think of it, who didn't?), Daddy loved him like a son. His horse trainer, Ray Spencer, has to be the nicest man in the world, fielding calls from Daddy at all hours of the night while continuing to bring in winners at the track.

Our sister Ann gets the Boorhem Medal of Honor for service over and above the call of duty. For the past five years, she has managed Daddy's business and been a primary caregiver, traveling to Shreveport weekly. Brother Ross gets the Boorhem Peace Prize for his calm, ever present, and patient handling of Daddy. Ross was Daddy's go-to guy at any hour of the day or night, including loading the entire TV schedule on his iPhone to tell Daddy what to watch every night.

We would have been wandering in the dark without the expert and loving guidance of our sister Beth, who works in the senior care field, and who walked us through every decision and every transition, with copious information, referrals, and willingness to be the point person for doctors and nurses.

I was the self-designated scribe for this journey and will be penning a best-seller soon about the life of Crusher Bill. We are counting on me winning the Pulitzer Prize and catapulting all of us to fame and fortune.

Sister Barbra and Brother Kevin and his wife Lyndsey were exempt from most duties due to geography and a new baby, but they were on every family call offering moral support and were with us in spirit on every trip to the farm.

When I said to myself that night, "Yep, Daddy, we'll give this thing a whirl, as long as we can!" that is exactly what we did. Each of us in our own way gave it a whirl with Daddy, helping with our talents, our expertise, our love, our stories, our support. The Year of Grace was just that for me: sacred, sad, hilarious, joyous, insightful, fun, cementing, and full of love.

Daddy's passing leaves a huge hole in our lives and in our hearts, and he will be deeply missed by his children, grandchildren, great-grandchildren, and many friends. They do not make them like him anymore. We have so appreciated your thoughts and prayers and kind words as we walked this last part of the journey with him. What an impact he had on so many!

William Boorhem did it his way. All day, every day of his life. He was eccentric, fearless, and human. Although terrified of him at times, we loved him madly.

His was the voice in my head that kept me working on and finally finishing my doctorate ("I'll probably be DEAD before you finish that thing"), and his will continue to be the voice in my head that moves me forward—"Life is for the living—don't waste it!"

Although he and I were often at cross purposes, that is water under the bridge. The Year of Grace was just that. I am so grateful for that year, for him, for the family he built, for being part of his zoom-zoom life, for the stories and memories that will be passed down through the generations.

And though I now know that he was not immortal, he will live in our hearts forever. And when I see him in my dreams, he will be dancing with the angels and raising hell in heaven. And down here, Daddy, we will live life, and we will not waste it.

Go, Daddy, go.

ABOUT THE AUTHOR

For someone whose dream was to be a Broadway star, Dr. Boorhem's career trajectory might seem a little strange. Although she lived for theatre in high school and college, she couldn't handle the "drama" and back-stabbing and soon dropped out to "go make money."

After ten years in the corporate world, she decided that wasn't for her either and took a U-turn back to school to finish her bachelor's, master's, and doctoral degrees, all in one fell swoop.

The next thirty years were spent in private practice as a therapist, teaching at the university level, consulting with nonprofit agencies, and leading a large youth-serving organization. Most recently, Dr. Boorhem co-founded It's Lonely at the Top! a professional leadership development program for female nonprofit CEOs.

Although Dr. Boorhem has published scholarly articles, this is her first book. Writing has been a constant in her life, however, with her chronicling opinions, stories, and observations in blogs, social media, newsletters, diaries, and letters. *The Year of Grace* was birthed from ongoing updates she posted on Facebook throughout the time she cared for her father.

A "Cliff-dweller for life," Dr. Boorhem has lived in Oak Cliff in Southern Dallas, Texas, for over thirty years. She has two grown daughters, one of whom is married, two large and rambunctious dogs, and a Maine Coon cat. She enjoys reading, solving NYT Crosswords, walking her dogs, doing nothing, practicing yoga, writing, and watching British TV.